FORERUNNERS: IDEAS FIRST FROM THE UNIVERSITY OF
MINNESOTA PRESS

Original e-works to spark new scholarship

FORERUNNERS: IDEAS FIRST is a thought-in-process series of
breakthrough digital works. Written ?
ished books, Forerunners draws on scl
ble blogs, social media, conference pl
the synergy of academic exchange. Tl
ing: where intense thinking, change, ε
scholarship.

Ian Bogost
The Geek's Chihuahua: Living with Apple

Andrew Culp
Dark Deleuze

Sohail Daulatzai
Fifty Years of "The Battle of Algiers": Past as Prologue

Grant Farred
Martin Heidegger Saved My Life

David Golumbia
The Politics of Bitcoin: Software as Right-Wing Extremism

Gary Hall
The Uberfication of the University

John Hartigan
Aesop's Anthropology: A Multispecies Approach

Mark Jarzombek
Digital Stockholm Syndrome in the Post-Ontological Age

Nicholas A. Knouf
How Noise Matters to Finance

Akira Mizuta Lippit
**Cinema without Reflection: Jacques Derrida's Echopoiesis and
Narcissism Adrift**

P. David Marshall
The Celebrity Persona Pandemic

Reinhold Martin
Mediators: Aesthetics, Politics, and the City

Shannon Mattern
Deep Mapping the Media City

Davide Panagia
Ten Theses for an Aesthetics of Politics

Jussi Parikka
The Anthrobscene

Steven Shaviro
No Speed Limit: Three Essays on Accelerationism

Sharon Sliwinski
Mandela's Dark Years: A Political Theory of Dreaming

The Celebrity Persona Pandemic

The Celebrity Persona Pandemic

P. David Marshall

University of Minnesota Press

MINNEAPOLIS

Portions of chapter 1 were published as "Stephen Colbert the Persona Is Ending—and I Will Miss Him," *The Conversation,* May 2, 2014; portions of chapter 2 were published as "The Cate Blanchett Persona and the Allure of the Oscar," *The Conversation,* February 26, 2014; chapter 3 was published as "Glamour Photography Makes Suburban Stars of Us All," *The Conversation,* December 9, 2013; portions of chapter 4 were published as "Celebrity Fakes—Where Porn Meets a Sense of Possession," *The Conversation,* December 12, 2013. Portions of chapter 7 were published as "Seriality and Persona," *M/C Journal* 17, no. 3 (2014), http://journal.media-culture.org.au. Portions of chapter 8 were published as "Intercommunication and Persona: The Intercommunicative Public Self," *International Journal of Interdisciplinary Studies in Communication* 10, no. 1 (2015): 23–31.

Published by the University of Minnesota Press, 2016
111 Third Avenue South, Suite 290
Minneapolis, MN 55401-2520
http://www.upress.umn.edu

The University of Minnesota is an equal-opportunity educator and employer.

To my wonderful wife, Sally, for all her love
and support and to the rest of my family:
my mother, Theo, and my children, Erin, Zak,
Julia, and Paul, for listening to my sometimes
rambling prewritten ruminations.
We are all personas in formation.

Contents

Introduction: Persona in Formation   1

1. Stephen Colbert Reveals His True Self   7

2. The Cate Blanchett Persona at the Oscars   14

3. Glamour Photography Democratizes Fame   19

4. The Total Exposure of Justin Bieber,
   Miley Cyrus, and Others   22

5. The T-Shirt Phenomenon in China   28

6. Politics of Recognition   36

7. Listicles and the Play of Klout   41

8. Seriality and Persona from
   Spock to Harry Potter   48

9. Intercommunication and Cultures
   of Surveillance   64

Conclusion: Pandemic Persona   78

References   85

Introduction:
Persona in Formation

THE CULTURAL CRITIC is often called upon to provide some type of summary of the contemporary moment. With all the disparateness of politics, artistic practice, changes in the flows of media, new media and forms of consumption, and the myriad transformations that have arisen from both science and technology, it is a difficult task—perhaps nearly impossible.

This collection is an attempt to distill at least one dominant trope that defines the contemporary cultural condition. The series of essays pieced together here is an exposé that explores the increasing fetishization of the construction of a public persona. The idea of fetish is useful in describing persona because it is important to see that persona is an accoutrement or mask added on to the self in order to achieve some sort of completion and satisfaction in the public world. Persona construction is not about the real "self," but it will have indices that link the individual to the persona. Persona is about a strategic form of public identity; but, more than any other moment, this persona construction—its fetish quality—has become pandemic in the contemporary moment.

If my distillation of the contemporary is accurate—that we have a pandemic obsession with constructing personas—it is important to see why this has arisen. What constellation of events, technologies, cultures, and industries has produced what could be called the constant preening of the presentation of the self? What are the critical changes that have allowed for this to emerge?

Some elements of the persona obsession come from longer historical cultural arcs. For instance, there are elements of consumer culture that have increasingly focused on the individualized production of the self, which at least identifies elements of the obsession that have grown and intensified for more than a century. We are invited to piece together a sartorial style each day that has some intersection with existing social, professional, and cultural categories and fields, but this style is also part of the organization of the contemporary that we must make this meaning real for us individually and personally for every day and for our movement through public (and private) and privatized spaces. Also, accompanying this personalization in consumer culture and the making of the public self has been an elaborate and intersecting media and entertainment system of communication that also celebrates forms of individuality. For more than two centuries, a celebrity system has developed that constructed a representative field of personalities that not only shaped our conceptions of significance but also were part of a newly permeable public sphere (Inglis 2016). Celebrities operated as a system of transferring value in a culture—they were entities that have been allowed to move into the highest echelons of the political, economic, and cultural elite. Their movement ultimately served as an ideological legitimation source that helped define the contemporary as open and accessible and, in some cases, democratic and meritocratic.

Thus the personalization of value via consumer culture and the recalibration of reputation and impact through the value of celebrity culture have laid the groundwork for what is the critical technological—and cultural—change that has shifted the contemporary moment to an obsessive focus on the public persona. Online culture has progressively led to an increasingly greater focus on the production of the self. From the early days of the World Wide Web, when people had "personal" websites, what had been emerging was a parallel world of mediatization of the self. The graphic quality of the Web meant that in progressive stages, the individual could produce a version of her own activities that resembled a newspaper, a magazine, and, by the time of YouTube in 2004, a television channel. Indeed, combinations of these forms advanced over the last twenty years of what I wrote about in the 1990s as the initial "graphic internet stage" (Marshall 1997) and blended into what became known as weblogs, or blogs, and videologs, or vlogs, in the early part of the twenty-first century.

Augmenting this mediatization of the self and the naturalization of this construction and production of a public self was the development of applications that made the process of the production of an online public self simpler and of more value. Although MySpace was one of the earliest of these types of online applications, Facebook gradually became one of the largest players in this space of production of the self. The personal value in this production was related to the networking structure of these applications. Whatever you posted became available to the "friends" that you had self-identified or had linked with you in some way. Public settings of information determined your wider mediatized self, while various privacy settings determined the inner micropublics that any individual Facebook user cultivated. Along with links to other elements of interests and likes that structured the meaning of the public individual through an array of social and cultural markers, Facebook and other social media sites have places and locations for the posting of photos, videos, comments, and interpersonal forms of exchange. In other words, whether through Facebook, Instagram, Google+, LinkedIn, Pinterest, or Tumblr, literally billions of people worldwide are producing public versions of themselves and monitoring those productions of the self daily.

As this system of the production of the public self has become normalized and naturalized over the last decade, it has led to a spectrum of the production of a public persona that in the past would have been an activity only engaged in by a quite limited celebrity and public personality culture. Thus there are now continuities in the production of public identities that move from the most celebrated to the teenager attracting followers and friends through his flamboyant posts (boyd 2014; Marshall 2014a).

The Justin Bieber persona captures much of this movement. In the opening sequence of the 2016 comedy movie *Zoolander 2* and its lampooning of fashion, Justin Bieber is being chased by assassins through the parkours-friendly backstreets of Rome. Ultimately, the assassins are successful, pummeling Bieber with hundreds of bullets. Left for dead, Bieber's last act is to post an image of his death pose on Instagram; as he is dying, he is choosing the best look along with the best shading as he keeps selecting and reselecting which image to post. Bieber in the movie is playing himself, and thus the role is a study of a celebrity still trying to manage his online image and persona personally until his last gasp. It portrays effectively in conveying that his "death" in the film would be welcome by many who consider Bieber's publicly visible activities in his real life of the last few years at minimum cringe-worthy.

In a larger sense of how social media are depicted in this film through Bieber, we can see how the constant and staged negotiation of identity is as much part of the most famed regular and everyday practices as it is for each of us.

Personas, thus, were once a form of mediatized construction produced for display and production in television, radio, film,

Death scene of Justin Bieber in *Zoolander 2* (2016).

and print media; in the contemporary moment, variations of this production are occurring across the social spectrum. The implications of pandemic persona culture are immense and in many ways still to be determined, but the production of a public version of the self is already transforming our work culture, some professions, and, definitively, our leisure and recreational lives.

This volume represents an analysis of the beginning stages of what I call a "presentational cultural regime," as opposed to the "representational cultural regime" that was privileged by our highly mediatized culture of traditional media. To capture this persona moment, the following essays identify the production of the self in different environments. Some of these analyses reveal the celebrity in action, but viewed with a lens of how it informs this production of a mask of identity. Celebrities often represent the best way to understand the highly constructed nature of a persona. Taking apart Stephen Colbert's fabricated identity or working out the posturing of an actress such as Cate Blanchett actually helps us makes sense of the pandemic construction of public identity and reveal its strategic nature. Investigating the bizarre world of celebrity fakes, where the blend of digital identity is possible, also reveals the risks of public personas more widely. Several of the essays describe the pedagogic connection of the celebrity world with the everyday construction of a mediatized identity. Glamour photography is explored as an engine of experimentation in mediatized identity for the suburban individual. Serial dramas offer a way to see how the consistency of public identity establishes a coherence that is at play in the most mundane social media presentation of the self. And it is always useful to look at the different ways that public identity is constituted in different regions, cultures, and nations—this is developed in the essay on comparative persona. I have ended this series of analyses with a conceptual piece on the persona emerging through the online industries—what I call the intercommunicative persona.

The contemporary moment is now filled with a new form of work: we are constantly laboring on the presentation of ourselves for public consumption. Visibility, reputation, impression management, and impact are at play as we work and labor on the production of our online and public personas. The value generated from this work—a kind of work that recent scholarship is labeling as self-branding—is quite difficult to calibrate for the individual but nonetheless is seen as a necessary self-production as one's sartorial style for moving through public spaces. The contemporary moment is a specular moment of the self where individual by individual, and ultimately, collectively, we are making and remaking our public personas. The sad truth of this persona production is that our labor is a massive information source that feeds the new structure of consumer culture, the new formation of advertising, and the new focused efforts to connect industries to help us construct smart public versions of ourselves.

1. Stephen Colbert Reveals His True Self

March 2015: Part I—
The Last Days of *The Colbert Report*

What happens when an actor who has built such an amazing persona must reveal a truer self?

In March 2015, *Breaking Bad* actor Bryan Cranston appeared on *The Colbert Report*. In many ways, this is not unusual. The program often has guests who are hyping their latest shows, and Cranston was no exception; he was starring as LBJ, the American president who succeeded Kennedy after his assassination, in the Broadway play *All the Way*. But Cranston, whose role in *Breaking Bad* was career defining, while answering a question about how he can act as President Johnson without just doing an impression of the man, cajoled Colbert by asking him whether he knows what that's like. For an instant, Colbert was invited to leave his parodic persona as a right-wing talk show host, an identity he has inhabited with ferocity since 2007. For an instant, Cranston asked an innocent question between two actors. The identity-confusion gap quickly closed, however, when Colbert shook his head no and denied any real version of himself to squeeze through.

Colbert with David Letterman on the *Late Show with David Letterman* with Twitter selfie on April 22, 2014. CBS and Twitter.

Even this stutter in a performance has a certain normalcy in the Colbert universe. After all, the pleasure of watching *The Colbert Report* is to revel in the absurdity of his positions, his over-the-top narcissism, and, ultimately, his more than playful parody of the Rush Limbaughs and Bill O'Reillys of the televisual world, and without doubt the entire entourage of *Fox News* reporters and anchors. The graphics that open the show and provide the segues between segments or "acts" have reconstructed like a parallel universe the American patriotic tilt of images that populate *Fox News*.

The alluring wrinkle in this performance is the lack of distance between Stephen Colbert and Stephen Colbert the performer of this role: he has no differentiated stage name. Because it is couched in the role of a television "host," and with even more effect, a news host, the reality effect is that much stronger. The audience inhabits a purgatory position between believing the incredulous comments by Colbert and believing that the real Colbert is entirely aware of the parody itself and that his true self is some polar opposite. Colbert commits to both the right-wing talk show host and—complicit through the perceived insincerity of the penetrating gazes, the double meaning of a raised eyebrow, or an over-the-top reaction and understanding the "inside" jokes—allows this second related persona to be there as part of the complete character.

Colbert's performance is so overwhelming and energized in its layers and masks of constructed "real" identity that it is hard to imagine him in any other way. The sad truth is that we have to now.

A week after this performance gap with Bryan Cranston, CBS announced that Colbert was to replace the retiring David Letterman as the host of the *Late Show.* The offer of this position to any comedian is one of the holy grails in American entertainment and is only rivaled by the NBC position of *The Tonight Show,* now hosted by Jamie Fallon.

Constructions of public identities work in interesting and parasocial ways with audiences. With Colbert, converting his public persona to a real television talk show host demands some sort of dropping of his current masked identity, which paradoxically is how his audiences and the public now perceive him. According to most reports, at least in a public sense, Colbert has only done this about six or seven times in the last eight years. In fact, Colbert has even fronted up to a congressional committee on immigration totally and completely in character.

Hosting the *Late Show* will produce a qualitatively different public persona. For one, while *The Colbert Report* persona ridiculed the actual operation of television itself via its home on Comedy Central, the *Late Show,* however defined by both light entertainment and comedy, is also much more closely identified with traditional notions of television and representation:

after all, it is the same network that gave us the most venerated figure of American television—Walter Cronkite.

Also, talk show hosts are traditionally the actual locus for the movement of information about public personalities from the private to the public. The "guests," who are generally incredibly well known, are there to reveal as much as to construct their public identities further. The host, interestingly, has generally been a pleasant, slightly humorous foil to this engagement in celebrity culture. But, at their core—whether the host is Johnny Carson, Jay Leno, David Letterman, Ellen DeGeneres, or Conan O'Brien—hosts are generally perceived to be portraying their true selves. For example, Carson embodied an urbane and laconic humor, while Letterman occasionally allowed his feigned disinterest to articulate his distance from his subjects and his humor.

So far, Colbert the person—to distinguish him necessarily from the actor and the character—is a very private individual who reveals very little publicly. We know he is a devout Catholic, we know he is married and had a difficult childhood in South Carolina, and we know he learned his approach to performance and comedy from working at Second City in Chicago after studying drama at Northwestern University. Up until now, that personal identity has not been a major force in his public persona. In fact, his totalizing role on *The Colbert Report* has led to the rare moment in our public culture where the private and the public are not blended and benefit from not being linked.

Perhaps Colbert represents a new form of public persona. His years as being an outspoken "citizen" Colbert who talked about the "nation" and performed right-wing outrage have allowed him to achieve something that the ancient Greeks celebrated: a total separation of private and public life. One inhabited a persona in politics and cultural pursuits, but this was unconnected to the home life and domestic conventions. Persona was the way one structured oneself for the outside world. It was meant to be fabricated, and this allowed for an engagement with politics and an engagement with public and professional life with a mask and a knowingness that there was a kind of rhetoric of position involved.

For more than two centuries, we have seen the inner self as a source for the public self: this was the pathway to truth and enlightenment and even democracy. The fabricated identity of persona was seen as a disguise and the mask of performance, a lie. Celebrity culture, with television talk shows being one of its stalwarts, has been all about revealing the private world that would get us closer to the truth. Even *The Colbert Report* was all about exposing the bizarre masks of identity of right-wing American cultural icons to get us closer to the truth. Identifying scandal identified those pathways to truth. One of the most influential thinkers of the twentieth century, Hannah Arendt, described this search for truth in the personal as one of the failings of our democratic culture as she recommended a return to the ancient tradition of acceptable public identities for political discourse (Arendt 1958).

Stephen Colbert, as he transitions from total persona to the real talk show host, will be expected to reveal a true self. He may shift these conventions as to what a talk show does and what its host embodies, but my intuition is that he will begin to resemble his predecessors and that the interesting experiment of the totally constructed public persona of *The Colbert Report* will become just a character that he plays occasionally. I will miss him—that persona whose name rhymed with report (the *t*'s are silent . . .).

February 2016: Part II—
The First Days of the *Late Show with Stephen Colbert*

In September 2015, Colbert did indeed take on the role of hosting the *Late Show*; but the new performance by Colbert became a new and very elaborate game of authenticity about his persona.

On one level, Colbert was no longer shackled by his clearly fictional *Colbert Report* character. In the first months of the new show, Colbert presented more earnest opinions, had forays into expressions around faith and Catholicism, and even expressed what in American terms could be described as a liberalist political posture. Augmenting this were further efforts to identify his own forms of pleasure in terms of music and interests. His opening monologues worked very hard at establishing this new, more personally "real" identity. At times, Colbert would show he was indignant—probably most prominently following the Paris terrorist attacks of November 13.

On another level, those programs over the same months showed a slightly new and controlled character that was dependent on the old Colbert. It is true that much of his writing team came from his previous program and that Jon Stewart of *The Daily Show* was listed as an executive producer of the new show. The *Late Show* with Colbert helming differentiated itself by its remarkable focus on politics, specifically presidential election politics. One of his first guests was Jeb Bush, and this was followed by visits by secretary of state John Kerry, Donald Trump, and Vice President Joe Biden—the list of politicos was endless. In other words, at least one-third of the guests actually resembled the content of the old *Colbert Report*. Colbert himself remained tightly controlled in dress and manner. What became evident is that not so much a real identity was emerging as Colbert progressed in his new role; what was developing was a new persona slightly mutated from his former "acting" position. His long role on *The Colbert Report* produced a patterned identity of politics as both funny and compelling. In addition, the shift in identity was to underline how "smart" and "clever" and even intellectual he was, and this smartness made him funny but distinctive from other late-night comedians.

Even more compelling about the new Colbert was a continuing obsession with role and persona, whether in his own monologues or with guests. Star actors such as the quality television series *The Affair*'s lead actress, Ruth Wilson, and the ubiquitous Morgan Freeman were grilled about how they maintained their roles and personas, which often led to insider-type jokes about how Colbert himself had held an identity for so many years (Samuels 2015). In his regular skit titled "Big Questions with Even Bigger Stars," Colbert plays with his new spiritual depthness and intelligence lying under the stars with major celebrities like Tom Hanks, Charlize Theron, and Bryan Cranston, pontificating planned banalities about apparently important, meaning-of-life questions. Cleverness around his persona is maintained even by his choice of innovators and entrepreneurs as guests—from Tesla's Elon Musk to PewDiePie and GoPro's Nick Woodman.

Colbert's morphing into a late-night host is thus not an example of revelation of the self. What is compelling about the role change is how the construction of a public persona has moved center stage as an object of scrutiny. Colbert, via humor and in his constrained way, is inhabiting this exploration of this changing public–private divide obsession in our contemporary culture.

2. The Cate Blanchett Persona at the Oscars

No one is ever who they purport to be. And I suppose I'm not interested in the gap between who we project socially and who we really are.

—CATE BLANCHETT

NOT LONG AFTER her Golden Globe appearance and win in February 2014 in the Best Actress category for her title role in Woody Allen's *Blue Jasmine,* Cate Blanchett confessed that she was clearly drunk during her acceptance speech: of course, it became an instant online viral meme. On the celebrity gossip site PerezHilton.com, a rolling gif of her drinking vodka out of a martini glass captures the moment in a way that blends the reality of the award show with her film role seamlessly. The gif is actually her performance in *Blue Jasmine* and not related to the Golden Globes night or her admission that she was "a couple of sheets to the wind" and that she "couldn't remember a lot" related to her acceptance speech. Indeed, the reaction to Blanchett's admission was not shock or horror—it was generally supportive. Her role as a free-falling former socialite in the film somehow made her "real" role of drunken, loquacious Cate an acceptable presentation of a public self, almost a pathway to making the movie just that little bit more authentic.

A star's public persona is a very tricky business. The relationship to the character she plays is always an interesting negotiation

Robert De Niro's transformations as Jake LaMotta in *Raging Bull* (1980).

for the actor. She moves from the constructed story of a film to something that is projected in the public world as more real. That public world forms her celebrity status even though it is also layered with constructions and fabrications via red-carpet appearances, talk show vignettes, publicity stills, and the unplanned images produced by paparazzi. Think back to Robert De Niro in Martin Scorsese's *Raging Bull* (1980), where he gained forty pounds to play the later life stages of the boxer Jake LaMotta.

De Niro gained incredible credibility as a devoted actor, which, along with his earlier work in *Taxi Driver* (1976), defined De Niro for the rest of his career as an intense (with an undercurrent of potential violence), hypermasculine persona. Even in his comedy performances—and here I am thinking of the Meet the Fockers film series as well as hints in his recent *Last Vegas* (2013) performance—the intensity remains. We know that De Niro is a method actor who completely invests in his past performances, and that level of commitment is what defines his economic value as much as his public persona for his future career, as it has for most of its past. Allowing your film characters to become constitutive of your bankable persona leads to what could be described as the "John Wayne syndrome"—an actor thoroughly typecast in his career, but also an actor who revels in that straitjacket because it defines his stardom and value in the industry.

How do we read Cate Blanchett now? With her current role—a role that presents a pathetic individual who, as an audience, we are drawn to and repulsed by—her broken-down life and her carriage at presenting a persona *within* the film try to hide that past reality. The performance makes Blanchett into an "actor's actor" because it plays with the veils of identity and is a study on how those fabrications can become more real and, in this role, more debilitating. Cate Blanchett's achievement because she has worked so visibly hard at showing and removing these veils of identity in the film has been recognized by many industry awards because it speaks to this industry of performance. She may very well receive the Oscar for this performance on persona itself.

Personas are complex projections and masks, and success sometimes is built when performances, whether in the recorded public world or in films, resonate with each other. The repertoire of Cate Blanchett is heavily defined by its connection to the craft of acting. Thus her five-year directorship of the Sydney Theatre Company builds well with her projection as an actor. Her past roles are heavily coded with strong and independent women. Thus her title characters as Queen Elizabeth I in two major films are as indicative of her strong roles as a villain in *Indiana Jones and the Kingdom of the Crystal Skull* (2008), her repeat performances as the ethereal but powerful and regal elf-queen Galadriel in Peter Jackson's *Lord of the Rings* and *Hobbit* films, and even a determined woman in *The Curious Case of Benjamin Button* (2008). Where she has positioned herself also fits into the legacies of Hollywood itself and its definition of independence and strength. Her Oscar-nominated role as Katherine Hepburn in *The Aviator* (2004) is particularly revealing in its defining the negotiated public persona of Cate Blanchett. Hepburn was a Hollywood legend but managed to create a persona of independence, strength, and quality that allowed her some autonomy in classic Hollywood. In a very active sense, Blanchett is working to assume that mantle, albeit in a changed global Hollywood and a changed and much more visible public culture and display. Like Hepburn, Blanchett has constructed a patrician image that is further augmented by her capacity to convey wealth and status via her use of British and American accents. Her role in *The Good German* (2006) expands that sense of acting mastery via accents and through filming in black and white, which casts back to a classic Hollywood aesthetic of film noir and perhaps Ingrid Bergman and Lauren Bacall. Blanchett's accent performance in *Blue Jasmine* in fact may be her greatest achievement in the film as it reveals both its constructed and contrived presentation of American wealth and its hints of the vulnerability of that presentation. Further adding to what could be called her elite prestige is her connection to glamour. Glamour represents the genuflection to the power of classic Hollywood and its construction of femininity. Through her recent $10.4 million endorsement contract to be the spokesmodel for Armani perfumes, she expresses classic beauty and the power of that image in the most constructed way. Apparently, before he died, Armani said that Blanchett "epitomises the woman for whom I design."

Too great a distance, too much of a patrician, is dangerous in this new Hollywood world. What makes Blanchett acceptable in this new public world is her Australianness and the valuable asset of having an inside–outside relation to Hollywood itself that also allows her to make fun of her constructed images as she inhabits them in her film performances and her posed elegance for Armani.

Despite all this synergy in a very successful public persona, there are always wrinkles in the presented self as it constantly moves from performance to a mediated public world of news and publicity. As the publicity and news coverage heated up in anticipation of Oscar night, Blanchett had to deal with the new accusations of sexual abuse leveled at her director Woody Allen. Without these accusations, Blanchett's work with Allen would provide even further cultural cache, particularly in Hollywood and its sometimes peculiar reading of quality; but at that moment, she had to answer to, deal with, and sometimes avoid the way that a scandal can derail the very strong currents that would further establish Blanchett's persona with an Oscar triumph. The usually in-control but available Cate Blanchett was a little more scarce for further media exposure as Oscar night approached.

Coda

Cate managed to pick up the Oscar for her role in *Blue Jasmine* and functioned as a momentary compromise in the shifting interpretations of the very private Woody Allen's mixed public persona and his filmic value. Needless to say, Allen was not a winner for director.

3. Glamour Photography Democratizes Fame

IN SHOPPING CENTERS AND MALLS across much of Australia and North America, a peculiar and particular type of photography business makes itself at home. It goes under a number of names and guises, but it is generally described as glamour photography. At the core of this particular business is creating images that make the everyday person feel extra-ordinary or what we call a "star."

One of these businesses, Starshots, with its sixteen franchised studios across Australia, is nicely nestled in the suburban landscape. It advertises itself in glossy posters in the malls themselves with provocative photos of subjects dressed in what could be described as naughty gear.

On its website, Starshots explains its basic philosophy. Through the "Starshot experience," the client is to be "pampered" with its "proven formula" of makeup, hairstylists, props, and accessories of a true studio photo shoot as they work to capture the "essence of you." In other words, they cater for the production of the individual into the star, and the star experience is as important as the end photo product. Naturally, as would happen with a professional magazine cover shoot, the added services of touch-up and digital image alteration are there to capture the "real you."

Glamour photography as an industry has an interesting lineage that may help explain its current location in the suburban mall. As Carol Dyhouse (2010), author of the book *Glamour: Women, History, Feminism,* proclaims, "Glamour is a slithery concept." It relies on its strong connection to the stars of classic Hollywood, where the notion of glamour and its associated fur, slinky dresses, and attitude were an expression of the modern woman negotiating her public place in the contemporary world. But it is also a soiled concept. Glamour photography, as the twentieth century progressed, became associated with what was called boudoir photography, as even the idea of glamour began to be connected to tackiness. The most public version of this kind of photography was the soft-core pornography promulgated by the mid- to late-twentieth-century magazine icons of *Playboy* and *Penthouse* (Nelson 2013; Checefsky 2008). The particular photographic studios that now promote glamour photography in the shopping malls are trying to sanitize this bedroom photography and make it much more associated with the production of ourselves as stars so that couples as much as women can feel good about their sensual selves.

But why now? What about the contemporary moment makes this form of photography commercially successful (and it generally is) and both kind of normal and popular?

This particular version of glamour photography has been building for the last fifteen years, just as the photography industry has gone through its greatest upheaval predominantly driven by digital photography. It is evident from at least American industry reports that there has been a general decline in both revenues and the number of commercial photo studios. The decline is not massive, but instead of growth, there is about a 10 percent shrinkage in the market. Simultaneous to this decline is the overwhelming reality that people are producing many more photos and distributing them regularly. Cameras are on every device, from phone to tablet to iPod and iPad, never mind digital cameras themselves. Their progeny—snapshots—are literally everywhere, and we only need to think of the 40 million images a day being uploaded to Instagram to know that this is a massive change.

So the industry has to react to this world that resembles the Brownie camera craze at the beginning of the 1900s, when everyone was an amateur photographer. It has to make the experience of professional photography more. Glamour photography thus attempts to do what reality television actually does: it offers the service of "celebrifying" the individual. The photographs produced are very likely only to remain in one's own household, but it has the potential to cross over and be thought as connected to the pantheon of star images that we see every day produced by our sophisticated entertainment industries. Glamour photographic studios are generalizing the "star experience" that is presented in tantalizing forms through television making stars from its talent and reality shows out of everyday people. Possessing that construction of value allows one's own body/self to be incorporated into the contemporary media system, even if it is only to capture the "look" of fame for one's own pleasure.

Starshots is not the only player in this world. Photography studios like the franchisable Verve cater to the "family" portrait and are expert at making their portraits distinctive and different in their clear appeal to the aesthetic of magazine photography. Their portraiture is a combination of Karsch and Annie Liebovitz; it is magazine cover photography for the middle class. Its slogan captures this intermediary role: "The beautiful images captured from your photography session are handcrafted into creative, original works of art." The experience of the studio draws you into a world of feeling significant and famed.

4. The Total Exposure of Justin Bieber, Miley Cyrus, and Others

IN 2014, an online and mainstream media frenzy circulated about the meaning of Miley Cyrus. What does it mean when she twerks with Robin Thicke at the VMAs, or what can we construe from a former Disney child star, now twenty years old, appearing nude in her video for the song "Wrecking Ball"? Or how should we interpret Lily Allen weighing in to the debate about how popular music demands salacious and provocative images in her salacious—and, for some, racist—commentary song and video "Hard Out Here"? In 2015, this morphed into the equally provocative scandal where private and exposing images pulled from mobile phones of stars like Jennifer Lawrence virally moved through the Internet. At the opposite extreme, the last few years have produced occasionally heated debate among fans and anti-fans of Justin Bieber that perhaps we have seen too much of the singer, too much of his antics and attempts to make the private and public collide on Instagram. All of these examples identify the ultimate debate about the new visibility and the breakdown of public and private in the contemporary moment. Even our stars appear to be hacked for wider and open viewing of their habits and proclivities.

All of these absolutely pale in comparison to a remarkably present practice online: celebrity fakes. Website after website, one can find images of the most famous in some of the most hard-core pornographic poses. One of these sites, Celebrity Fake,[1] constructs a complete archive of thousands upon thousands of celebrities organized by name and country of fame. Miley Cyrus, along with other Disney alumni, such as Selena Gomez, is remarkably prominent and linked to the most popular on the site's home page, but the sheer number is unbelievable. Miley alone is found in 432 of these fake pornographic poses. No one is spared, and very few are sacred: there are 182 images of Princess Diana, 36 of fifty-something film actress Annette Bening, and 195 of the tennis star Maria Sharapova. No country is overlooked, from Albania to Zimbabwe. In listings for Australia, stars Cate Blanchett is reformed in 124 poses, Julia Gillard in 6, Kylie Minogue in 524, Libby Trickett in 3, and so on for more than 150 famous Australian women. This website is far from alone. A Google search under the phrase "celebrity fake porn" returns 37.3 million sites; using the term "celebrity porn" generates 170 million sites; and "celebrity porn sites" produces a list of 60.5 million links.

This phenomenon of celebrity fake porn is hard to fathom and at the very least intriguing to analyze. First of all, one would expect that the circulation of false images of very famous people would generate a torrent of lawsuits. After all, these famed individuals have spent years constructing their public personas and built fortunes related to their public identities, and one would think these same individuals would be outraged sufficiently to generate suits and litigation. For decades, scandal and celebrity magazines have been pursued by celebrities

1. http://cfake.com/home.

with some success. Impersonation is generally prosecuted by stars, and these images are putting their faces on other women's bodies, thereby producing a form of impersonation. Recent examples when stars have prosecuted impersonators include

Tom Waits successfully suing Opel, a GM-owned car manufacturer, for using a sound-alike gravelly voice to accompany its television commercials

Lindsay Lohan unsuccessfully suing E-Trade, a financial services company, for a baby called "Lindsay" in their 2010 Super Bowl–released commercial[2] who was called a "milkaholic"

now deceased Robin Williams pursuing the prosecution of a man impersonating him for financial gain at events in Texas

Even in Australia in 2015, Greens Senator and politician Sarah Hanson-Young is advanced with some success in suing *Zoo* magazine for publishing a photoshopped lingerie-clad image of her in a rather bizarre, tasteless, and obviously humorous campaign to find the hottest asylum seeker.[3]

Nonetheless, it is difficult to find any lawsuits against fake celebrity porn sites. One of the key reasons around this might be the awkward position celebrities inhabit in the public world. In most legal jurisdictions, such as the United States, although not in all, it is permissible to parody or satirize a public individual, and this allows the use of an identity in this way. Famous impersonators, such as Rich Little, were seen as entertainers. Will Ferrell's brilliant 2009 parody of George W. Bush interviewing himself[4] is certainly worth protecting

2. https://www.youtube.com/watch?v=5QS9rIZcjaw.

3. http://www.pedestrian.tv/news/arts-and-culture/greens-senator-sarah-hanson-young-to-sue-zoo-weekl/1b563c4e-c124-43f7-8d89-3740765909ee.htm.

4. https://www.youtube.com/watch?v=ikMKJwbMQ_M.

from litigation. What this means is that celebrities operate with slightly different rules in terms of the privacy of their identities—to a degree, their personas are in the public domain. In some ways, they can protect what might be called "personality rights" from exploitation at the hands of corporations and nefarious individuals. Making litigation difficult are two other factors. First, an image is generally owned by the photographer or his agency, and it is at least partially up to these parties to initiate legal action; thus celebrities may not be the starting point for lawsuits. Second, perhaps it is simply embarrassing for celebrities to draw attention to celebrity fake porn—after all, it is their faces that have been used, and to draw further scrutiny might be seen as further sullying reputations and images. From a legal standpoint, the websites make it very clear that the images are fake, making advancing a defamation case more difficult and even opening American First Amendment defenses to failure. The end result for the celebrity is an inordinate focus on what she would not want people to associate with herself.

As this legal inertia continues, there is no question that the universe of celebrity fake porn is expanding. One of the elements of this online phenomenon is that it is partially driven by user-generated content. Many YouTube videos guide individuals on how to use Photoshop to make "celebrity fakes," as DazTutorials does,[5] shading images to blend them together seamlessly. Other YouTube videos provide point-by-point instruction in how Photoshop can be used to remove clothing from an electronic image. This uploading of Photoshop production techniques of celebrity fakes by "amateurs" is encouraged by the key sites; moreover, these sites also en-

5. https://www.youtube.com/watch?v=X0w0CKXK1hk.

courage users to "request" new celebrity subjects to be made into celebrity fakes. It is also important to realize that celebrity fake porn is a potential major entry point into online pornography and serves to link many pornography sites as users move through images. In other words, celebrity fakes do what celebrities do at red-carpet events: they attract attention, and that attention is valuable for both the website and those linked to that website, merely replicating the way the online advertising and promotional economy operates.

This brings us to the last two key questions: what is the particular fascination with celebrity fake porn, and why now? Although there have been precursors to this celebrity pornography, with magazines such as *Celebrity Skins* or nude profiles of very famous celebrities appearing as far back as Marilyn Monroe in magazines such as *Playboy,* Vanessa Williams in *Penthouse,* or Paris Hilton more recently in *FHM,* the nature and dimensions of this phenomenon are quite different. As with most pornography, the fabricated graphic images presented are generally of women, with much less than 5 percent of all the images those of male public personalities. The target users—given that the images of famous men predominantly resemble gay male pornography—appear to be male. It is also different than the regular and tired phenomenon of what used to be called the "sex tapes" immortalized by Rob Lowe many years ago and expanded through the activities of drawing attention to what would be described as scandalous and sometimes illegal activity. This practice has been expanded and utilized to maintain the attention of the celebrity press by icons such as Paris Hilton and Kim Kardashian (see Maplesden 2015). To a degree, Miley Cyrus's efforts at defining herself as an adult and not a child through her videos, her twerking, and her provocative comments are at least part of this same construction of scandal and attention seeking that is ever present in contemporary entertainment culture.

Celebrity fake porn is in some ways much more mundane and ordinary. It is clearly a play in the world of private and public. It allows its audience to take what is part of the public world and migrate it into a private world. This migration is more than the tawdry use of pornography for sexual pleasure. It represents a form of possession of a public figure, a fantasy belief in the capacity of complete revelation and exposure of the public personality. This is its tonic for the user. The images themselves are very often obscene and degrading in their graphic bodily detail, and this identifies a further form of possession and ownership that is heightened because of the fame and value of the personality.

For the celebrity, because porn still represents something hidden and perhaps undiscussed publicly, celebrity fakes remain an underworld. Online culture, in its capacity to distribute and its encouragement of user generation, works very differently at producing an alternative form of public culture, a culture that presents new challenges to protecting one's image. Celebrity fake porn is at an interesting intersection of private and public, manipulation and attraction, which makes it of particular interest in an era when greater exposure of all of us online has become more and more normal. With 40 million images posted daily on a site such as Instagram, the celebrity fakes phenomenon is another example of the quite dramatic change in public and private culture that online culture has fostered. Celebrities are getting used to this world of image and potential manipulation more quickly than the rest of us; at least for the moment, celebrities en masse are ignoring these violations of the self.

5. The T-Shirt Phenomenon in China

TRAVELING—at least for me—always produces a tension between the familiar and the strange.[1] An airport, for instance,
classically fulfills this duality. As you meander through Dubai,
London Heathrow, Hong Kong, Shanghai, Tokyo, Melbourne,
or Singapore airports, the shop names cater to the familiar
quality of international brands that you can also readily identify
in shopping malls and city centers wherever you live. You will
see Valentino or Lacoste or the bag shop Coach interspersed
with a Swarovski and a Prada. The faces of these brands also
provide a comforting community of images. I think I have seen
Hugh Jackman's face with his Montblanc pen in every one of
the ten international airports I have visited in the last year. This
array of international personalities and brands links with the
structured flow of airports—the signs that point to gates, the
general patterns of how people negotiate the airport experience and safely depart by air or on the ground.

1. I want to thank the School of Journalism and Communication at
CCNU in Wuhan for their support and their graduate student interest in
my work, in particular, from Ms. Wang Dongfang.

Hugh Jackman in Montblanc's advertisement—everywhere you want to be.

However, airports also situate you in the strange. Even basic rules shift from country to country; for example, walking on the left or the right or relative and newly appropriate proximity to others are things that still churn at airports as the new regimen of deportment of self only begins to shift your own individual behavior. The different dominant language is the most obvious example of the shift, but there are others. Sidling alongside the recognizable faces of stars and their associated brands are other "personalities" that by their size and position *should* be recognized. The Emir of the United Arab Emirates is ubiquitous in the Dubai airport, sometimes as a cut-out that resembles a movie star in a video shop, sometimes on large, glossy billboards. In different

Asian cities I have passed through, there is an array of "famous" people whom I can spot by their visibility and evident glamour via images and posters in public places like airports, but I just can't identify them. These are the obvious differentiations in how the strangeness of new places is sometimes presented to us: we can't read the public personality system. We know the signifiers of the famous—in some way, these have become internationalized as syntactically recognizable codes of value—but their identities are a mystery.

Understanding the familiarity and strangeness of place for the traveler can be characterized in many more ways than acknowledging how the public personality system is sometimes recognizable, sometimes translatable, and sometimes entirely foreign. Nonetheless, thinking through the way in which public personas are differently constituted opens new views to a particular culture and the way that it presents itself publicly.

In the last few years, I have had the opportunity to observe a little microcosm of how persona is presented publicly in China that has helped me understand how persona can be quite differently constituted in different settings. As a distinguished foreign expert at Central China Normal University (CCNU) in Wuhan, I lived on the pretty campus along with about twenty thousand students and university staff and their families. In some sense, it was a village embedded in a very large city with a series of gates connecting the two. People wandered around the campus's tree-lined streets from class to canteen, from basketball courts through gardens and back to their apartments.

Like international airports, the university resembled other universities around the world and presented a familiar enough terrain for someone like me to feel, if not at home, at least comfortable in my capacity to navigate. Of course, there were differences that made it difficult to decipher and, at times, a puzzle.

One of the most interesting differences was what I thought was a peculiar dress style. Thousands of students chose to wear T-shirts with English words prominently proclaiming something. I know this presentation of self no doubt produced a bigger effect on me. I couldn't read Mandarin, so much of the textual world of the campus, and the city as well, was opaque to me. And, surprisingly, in the midst of this Chinese campus, where almost no English was spoken and, likewise, I was relatively mute, were all these words on T-shirts "speaking" to me as students walked by me.

What was equally surprising to me was that many of the expressions on these shirts were nonsensical or at least challenging to interpret. Here is just a short list of what I read and recorded:

Shoot Free Shoot now

U gut. I gut

Dirty Poet Scum

Acne Studios 23

Watch Your side

More Respect Less Attack

Eyes without the cloudiness

SAT IS FACTION

Play Hide and Seek with me

Welcome to the Hatmptons

Woman is Beautiful. Woman's fashion is very good

Mastering black. Commended garçons

The range of these English expressions was truly amazing, and I began collecting them and trying to divide them between male and female wearers. Interspersed with these more bizarre expressions were the usual brands, such as Adidas, Coca-Cola and Seagram's 7, and some shirts appeared to be identifying where the individual had traveled (e.g., "I heart Italia"). In addition, quite a number attempted to express things in French ("Mo Amour Paris"). Whether in English or French, incorrect spelling was regular.

It became clear through conversations with some of the students with whom I had the opportunity to discuss this T-shirt phenomenon that, more or less, students were generally unaware of the English meanings. In other words, young women conveyed that they had chosen the letters and designs because they looked good. In general, the foreign words were a sign of some value, a kind of low-level reading of "cool," and the English meaning was meaningless. For some, it was linked to the culture of "cute," and it was less the words than the other images of cute anime-inspired animals that were often also on these tops that made students both buy and wear them. In contrast, it was exceedingly rare to see Chinese characters or scripts on any clothing.

Comparative Persona Analysis

It is very important to admit that the complexity of how a public persona is constructed and its dependence on specific national, regional, and ethnic, if not family, dimensions mean that my ability to decipher this T-shirt phenomenon in Wuhan, China, is limited and is much more a considered conjecture about what it means. The reading of the public display of the self identifies the differentiation that is at play in the way that individuality and its public presentation operate in different settings. Some of these factors are what I would identify as "extrinsic" qualities. For instance, students wearing T-shirts is something that you would see in many countries, and it becomes a means of identity display transnationally. Indeed, the wearing of English-texted T-shirts is something you would see throughout Asia in some form or another. For example, in Japan, this externalization of Western texts is very much explicitly related to international brand names, and the text itself becomes a moniker of taste and value attached to commodity culture. This outward expression by individuals of brand culture is making the public self part of transnational flows of value: it is an extrinsic quality.

In the Wuhan instance, the use of English is both an extrinsic and "intrinsic" quality of persona. Appealing to a foreign language to express the self publicly is interesting and only appears to be extrinsic. Because the actual words used and the expressions generated are not necessarily important, there is something inherently intrinsic occurring here as well.

Individuality in the new China is in some form of fluctuation. Industrially and economically, China has allowed a massive accumulation of wealth to occur as individuals are now celebrated for their business acumen and their capacity to both produce and sell Chinese products worldwide. In some ways, this is a celebration of entrepreneurialism that, if read from a Western context, would be a clear reflection of a freedom of the individual. It would be an extension in some way of what has generally been called neoliberalism and would thus articulate a neoliberal subjectivity.

In the Chinese context, and related to its own history of how individuality is positioned, this individuality is not quite the same, though it is influenced by neoliberalism within the context of internal Chinese politics and identity tensions. Hence we need this comparative work on persona to read the way that individualism is expressed in China. Hong-Mei

Li (2010, 145) has identified this as the move from *cheng-fen,* with its origin in class and family value and prestige that was instrumentally part of the Cultural Revolution and its celebration of humbleness in heroism, to *shenjia,* where the value of the individual becomes associated with money, assets, and the notion of the brand.

The peculiar T-shirt phenomenon, then, could be read as an interesting negotiation of this new tension in Chinese culture expressed through its youth. The T-shirts themselves help present a highly differentiated population with individualized forms of expression, which contrasts with the past's more regulated sense of dress, or even a form of counterpoint to the military dress that youth have to inhabit periodically in China. They also point to some international and outward-looking quality in the way that a public identity is made. In this way, they are a subtle and underplayed presentation of the branding of the self in the Chinese context. As I mentioned earlier, the focus on brand names is quite limited in this public display relative to other cultures. The T-shirts themselves emerge from many small T-shirt manufacturers and are print-screened individually or in small groups to service this display of a massive variety of different T-shirts. Moreover, the texted T-shirt is generally a very cheap article of clothing, even in the Chinese context: it is designed to be temporary and a signal of quiet and perhaps even apolitical difference.

So, the CCNU student T-shirt phenomenon to an outside observer is a concatenation of a consumer self and a productive/enterprising self. It is presented publicly in an era when there are different relationships between the public, the private, and the intimate that are occurring in the wider sweeps of Chinese and transnational culture and are rippling through the new uses of online culture and social media.

Along with the general experience of travel, the T-shirt phenomenon is an example of how we need to develop carefully comparative persona research and thinking. The intrinsic and extrinsic qualities occur both in the way celebrity culture (see, e.g., Edwards and Jeffreys 2010) is depicted in different settings and in how public comportment of the self is normalized and routinized.

6. Politics of Recognition

Preamble

In what Stuart Hall has called the Kilburn Manifesto, he outlines a need for a new attack on the current unique configuration of capital and the havoc it is wreaking on social and political life. Hall suggests,

> Market forces have begun to model institutional life and press deeply into our private lives, as well as dominating political discourse. They have shaped a popular culture that extols celebrity and success and promotes values of private gain and possessive individualism. They have thoroughly undermined the redistributive egalitarian consensus that underpinned the welfare state, with painful consequences for socially vulnerable groups such as women, old people, the young and ethnic minorities.
>
> Is celebrity culture simply an ideological support of new capital?

With his Kilburn Manifesto, Hall is looking to form a new political coalition, one that recognizes that the past welfare state is inadequate and that the current configuration of capital post–Global Financial Crisis is actually advancing on the dismantling of further efforts of social support. He indicates that capitalism, instead of suffering a retreat, as it had done under other massive threats to its organization, for example, the

Great Depression (which led as a consequence to the New Deal and the social welfare state), nothing is building coherently in the polis to counteract these forces. Despite interesting movements and forces, none has cohered to challenge this dimension of capitalism.

And wedded to this, from Hall's perspective, is a celebrity culture that supports it—that doesn't allow the emergence of collectives in its celebration of the public person and possessive individualism. So here is the question: is this kind of popular culture leadership really producing a culture that cannot organize, that cannot produce a different constitution of a public and relies instead on its divisions based on the hyperindividual model of celebrity?

The answer is classically yes and no—we do have a culture that pushes each of us to present ourselves, to draw attention to ourselves and differentiate ourselves. We could use all sorts of monikers to describe this organization of not the self so much as the public self. I am leaning toward terms derived from Raisborough (2011) and her book *Lifestyle Media and the Formation of the Self,* where she talks about the push to recognition. We are living in a recognition culture, one that I have described as a "specular economy" in some of my writing (Marshall 2010b), that draws our own attention to how we present ourselves to others. Anthony Giddens (1991), in his description of late modernity, identifies that our contemporary culture organization has intrinsic and extrinsic dimensions: the intrinsic is how we are focused on self-improvement, which manifests in efforts such as cosmetic surgery, fitness, and economic well-being, and even in the practice individualized religions that rely less and less on traditional culture's notions of connection and solidarity. Authors such as Micki McGee (2005) and Alison Hearn (2013) have taken this focus on the self as being a way that the self is now branded across our culture—inescapably linked to the system of capital in its individualization—and also linked to a systemic sense of our own inadequacies and of making the self in new, improved ways that rely on the material and social psychology of consumer culture. I will come back to elaborate on this further in a moment. Giddens's extrinsic reading of late modernity points to our outwardly focused qualities—those where the dimensions of globalization are part of our every day and the differences in the way we are drawn to these larger dimensions are equally an assault on what might be defined as more traditional conceptions of collective identity.

What has expanded since Giddens wrote those dimensions and challenges to the self in 1991 have partially been taken up by those such as McGee (2005), Banet-Weiser (2012), and Christine Harald (2013), and it is clearly a sense of how self-branding in its structure is dependent on a global anxiety of inconsistency and a sense of perpetual inadequacy that are as much a part of work culture as the way we present ourselves in and through our leisure. What Giddens could not have captured in his reading in 1991 was the emergence of the techniques and technologies of expression that have allowed individuals to map themselves—really present themselves—not necessarily globally but publicly. In the public presentation of the self, there is the sense and sensibility of the local connections and the global programs and applications intersecting. Thus Facebook, as much as its origins are American, is global in its application to the needs of users to express themselves to others; in this way, it resembles the telephone system in its facilitating a new sociality. To link them to the past and position them in their present and future, I have called these social network applications that are associated with the Internet, computers, and other apparatuses of mobile connection *technologies of the social*. These technologies of the social thus resemble apparatuses such as television—in other words, they draw people together, they create collective experiences, and they provide some of the tools through which we imagine connection (what I would call here our techniques and ideologies, where the collective "we" is effectively used and accepted). However, these new technologies of the social—such as Facebook, Instagram, and Twitter—position the individual differently in the chain of communication, in the organization of engagement, and in the play of connection. They privilege the individual starting point in an elaborate intercommunication chain to constructed micropublics or networked publics. This is different, this is new, and it is the technologies that have been producing a new sociality. Think of it this way: Lady Gaga has tens of millions who follow her on Twitter; I have hundreds, but we are on a spectrum of presentation of the self. Both of us are producing our personas for publics. It is not so much that the individual starting point—whether it be a focus on celebrity or a focus on a friendship circle on Facebook—takes away the power of the collective; it is that the public individual—modeled very much on the celebrity presentation of the self—produces a different and valued politics of the social and the collective. Our objective, then, is to see how these various dimensions of a new public individuality intersect and produce and foster a shifted politics and a new cultural affect that engenders the play of the individual self so closely to a new politics, a new public, and a new cultural collective. Harnessing this specular economy, building its affective dimensions via the public individual, via the persona, is the challenge—is really my challenge to comprehend it, perhaps facilitate it, read it for all its different flows of power, responsibility, and collective formation. It is an anxiety-ridden culture, but it is a different culture that builds from a new constitution of use of technology to establish the relationship between the individual and the social.

We are in an era of the politics of recognition—there is a pragmatic dimension, and there is an interesting social and psychological dimension that actually shifts our politics in novel ways that can be recaptured into forms of social power. Stuart Hall, you are correct: it is a kind of possessive individualism that celebrity, as it intersects with the pervasive culture of public persona, elevates; but the social dimensions of the technologies of the social are underexplored as these personas intersect and build their mutual forms of recognition. I find the directions of this politics not clearly aligned with the past, not clearly unharnessable, but demanding a much closer look at how we reach for recognition and for different configurations of collective experience that establish a quite different political and public sphere.

7. Listicles and the Play of Klout

WE RANK AND WE RANK SOME MORE—this does sound some-what disgusting, unless we think of the "other" meaning of rank: it is a truism of our contemporary moment that we are constantly attempting to establish ratings and rankings. Where does this desire to rank come from? What is its value? Why has it intensified so dramatically in recent years?

First, who does these rankings?

One of the interesting phenomena of magazine publishing of the last twenty years is that it has worked to corner the market on ranking, but with far from complete success. Think of the term Fortune 500, and we are drawn to *Fortune* magazine, where the top five hundred corporations are listed. Similar efforts have been employed by *Rolling Stone* magazine to rank popular music albums, adding aesthetics to the efforts of *Billboard* magazine's sales-derived Top 100 format, or perhaps for a more contempo-rary feel, iTune song downloads. *Forbes* magazine's own fortune and reputation rises and falls with its series of rankings of public personalities that have become somewhat of a gold standard for the determination of individual rankings. We have the top one hundred most influential celebrities, the rich list, the individu-al country celebrity lists, the most powerful women list, and so on. *Time* magazine's Person of the Year award indirectly constructs a ranking of the also-rans, and it is awaited with some anticipation each December, but its organization of rankings of influence occupies many issues throughout the year. Indeed, one would have to identity that one of the most prominent and powerful forms of click-bait on the Internet is to include one's information in a top five, ten, or twenty ranking. These forms of popular online communication are now called *listicles*.

Higher education has become increasingly influenced by rankings as they have moved from national contexts to world comparisons. *U.S. News and World Report* pinned some of its principal earnings on its American college ranking issues and catalogs, which have served to position the relative reputations of the sixteen hundred or so colleges and universities in the United States in a clear pecking order. Institutional ranking of universities has certainly expanded: the first global ranking of universities was conducted by Shanghai Jiao Tong University in 2003, with its publication of *Academic Rankings of World Universities* (Hazelkorn 2011), and was quickly matched by the *Times QS World University Rankings* in 2004.

American Top 40 is a long-running effort to maintain the pulse of American culture, while efforts by *Top of the Pops* in Britain or *Countdown* in Australia have provided a similar service via television—at least historically. At the end of the year, similar lists identify the top news events ranked in terms of their power to affect us. Along with the *New York Times* bestseller lists and a host of online ranking services that are determining relative sales and purchases of things, we are used to being ranked. For instance, my first book, *Celebrity and Power,* has an Amazon Best Sellers rank of 1,024,080, which of course is suitably humbling.

Rankings quite simply occur everywhere: they are part of our online search behavior as we look for how Google has ranked via its PageRank (see Hillis, Petit, and Jarrett 2013) system. Recipes are ranked and numbered; movies are listed into top ten categories. IMDb even blends the present and the past in its list of Top 100 Actors in American cinema as number 1 (!!!) Woody Allen rubs shoulders with number 6 Humphrey Bogart and number 78 Brad Pitt.

Increasingly, we are seeing the expansion of rankings that are calibrating individuals as much as institutions or products. The origins of this kind of calibration have built from individual sports primarily and major league drafts in some of the major professional team sports. For instance, tennis and golf have maintained elaborate international rankings for some time. The men's Official World Golf Ranking has been generated since 1986, while the men's Association of Tennis Professionals (ATP) and the Women's Tennis Association have maintained a world ranking system since 1973 and 1975, respectively. The reasons for rankings are to determine appropriate entry levels for tournaments that are fair and justified: from the earliest stages, the ATP identified that it was a "computer ranking system" to give it the aura of both objectivity and infallibility. By extension, and for "seeding" purposes, official rankings now populate these same sports (along with squash, table tennis, racquetball, handball, swimming, and athletics) well down into the most junior of ages: Florida, for instance, ranks its tennis players in the eight and under category. Australia has a tennis ranking system that does not differentiate the various divisions and moves from the most highly ranked professional to the most lowly ranked ten-year-old who has played a "ranking" tournament.

The systems and structures of ranking people have been built on different metrics with elaborated matrices of values and hierarchies. In the world of academia, one can see that citations define impact in a field and sites and programs such as Google Scholar build on their past ability to rank to express the relative value and rank of a given scholar. It is important to understand that Google Scholar is defined in terms of the individual "scholar" as much as the production of research. The capacity to build algorithms that in their intersection provide the ability (however flawed) to quantify prestige is moving through our various fields and professions. This capability to measure reputation depends on individuals' publicizing themselves through online means. Thus a Facebook profile, an Academia.edu account, a LinkedIn account, an Instagram presence, and membership among the Twitterati are also avenues to establish relative reputation. Social media are not only building in terms of sheer numbers, they are also building in terms of critical masses of categories of public selves that are known, identifiable, and thus *relationally* a way to measure prestige. The smaller social media networks, such as Academia.edu or even ResearchGate, are the vanguard of micropublics where prestige can be measured with greater accuracy. Thus there are not only the clustering of friends and followers but also specialized "leaders" of friends and followers in different disciplines, interests, professions, activities, and pastimes. Gamers embraced this system of prestige ranking perhaps before other groups because of their online culture but also because of the often close relationship between sport (and its associated ranking) and many games in terms of clear hierarchies of achievement.

Clearly connected to and emerging from this focus on public reputation and prestige is Klout, an online program that allows one to see one's impact calibrated and compared. Klout claims that it measures influence via surveying Twitter, LinkedIn, and Facebook in particular, but of course, its techniques, calibrations, and metrics are a secure form of intellectual property that the company maintains in the tradition of Google's always-improving PageRank system. On its site, it is working to monetize influence by providing "perks" to influencers as it labels those at the top of lists. Klout is also working to draw people to the application and site as a form of online traffic and thereby build on the power of current intercommunication industry and social media players such as Facebook and Twitter.

On the Pulse site of Klout, rankings and lists in various aspects of popular culture have proliferated: the most influential on Broadway or the top nongovernmental organizations are among those ranked. Even the most visible and influential scientists are listed and ranked. Klout is in a very real sense populating and colonizing the "market" of rankings and lists and presents an open challenge to their value and the presumed authority of traditional magazines.

The tendency to rank and position people is expanding. This expansion is part of the presentational media era, where position and rank are part of a more individualized contemporary culture supported by technologies of the social and, specifically, where online connections begin to establish relative value, relative influence, and perhaps relative potential power. In some ways, it is a cloying desire to be noticed, where a ranking helps establish internal and external markers of self-esteem, and Hearn and Shoenhoff (2016) as well as Marwick (2013; 2016) get very close to comprehending this "influencer" culture. With Klout and other forms of ranking, it is the connections that people possess and maintain—we could call these "friends" in Facebook language, "followers" in the Twitterverse, and now "influencers" in Klout's efforts to hierarchize—that help build profiles and reputations. They are affective personal connections and links that intersect with other affect clusters and thereby build what could be called micropublics: danah boyd (2011) has described these same connections as "networked publics," but in this ranking of value, we have the reassertion of hierarchies that begin to resemble the way representational media forms (film, television, radio, newspapers, and magazines) produced their celebrities and public personalities for most of the last century.

What is privileged in this new form of presentation of the self and calibration of the value of connection to the formation of a connected micropublic is the ability, first of all, to connect usefully; second of all, to exchange information effectively; third, to converse knowingly and receptively; and fourth and finally, to provide open-ended pathways to others to continue and maintain these developed connections. What is less clear in many of the Klout calibrations is if the quality of the form of intercommunication that is exchanged is somehow determined. By what can be discerned, the measurement of the ranking is determined by the power and influence of the range of people with whom you are connected and with whom you maintain regular forms of exchange. Klout underlines a new spatiality of influence, where those closer to other sources who have large numbers of followers and friends by appropriately connected associations become more identified with this form of social power.

The proliferation of both ranking and presenting the self publicly is insinuating itself into the professions and activities susceptible to a prestige economy structure. The capacity to build algorithms to index and map influence and to individualize those mappings is expanding. Moreover, these techniques of providing elaborate interconnected but also hierarchical matrices of influence are also critical to a changed consumer culture that is now more reliant on these smart "reading/ calibrating" technologies of the public self. Thus rankings are just around the corner in the academic world and will be organized around individuals as opposed to institutions. Similarly, the medical and legal professions will begin to have connected rankings to their specializations of knowledge and expertise that will partially be determined by relative and influential online presence and networking. Those professions and activities that are most associated with the manipulation of knowledge and ideas for applied purposes are on course for greater use of rankings and ratings.

How should this expanding world of individual ranking be met? Well, one countertechnique is to develop better ways of ranking and to have universities take the lead in developing these metrics of constructing individual value in a way that is not conjoined to a promotional culture of other products and services, as is the case for the intercommunication industry of social media and the "accounting of activity" that has become the basis for much of its perceived and real economic value. This kind of project requires the building of a slightly different network of research, one well connected to the disciplines and professions, but also one that is reliant on the tools of information science and econometrics: what is interesting is that any of a large number of universities have all of these forms of expertise in place. Interestingly, some of the largest publishing houses are beginning to service the need to rank at least for universities. Taylor and Francis's ownership and expansion of the influence of the Web of Science and the Social Science Citation Index are exercising their own clout with a C across that part of our professional academic world obsessed with rankings.

8. Seriality and Persona from Spock to Harry Potter

THE FICTITIOUS is a particular and varied source of insight into the everyday world. The idea of seriality—with its variations of the serial, series, seriated—is very much connected to our patterns of entertainment. In this essay, I want to begin the process of testing what values and meanings can be drawn from the idea of seriality into comprehending the play of persona in contemporary culture. From a brief overview of the intersection of persona and seriality as well as a review of the deployment of seriality in popular culture, the chapter focuses on the character–person-actor relationship to demonstrate how seriality produces persona. The French term for character—*personnage*—will be used to underline the clear relations between characterization, person, and persona that have been developed in the recent work by Lenain and Wiame (2011). *Personnage,* through its variation on the word *person,* helps push the analysis into fully understanding the particular and integrated configurations between a public persona and the fictional role that an actor inhabits (Heinich 2011).

Several qualities related to persona allow this movement from the fictional world to the everyday world to be profitable.

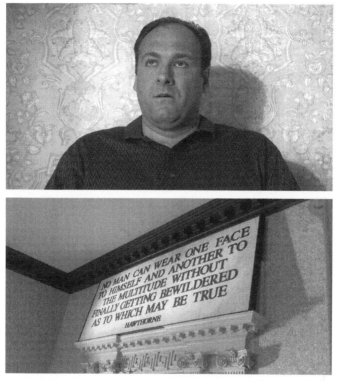

No man . . . can wear one face to himself and another to the multitude, without finally getting bewildered as to which one may be true." Nathaniel Hawthorne, *The Scarlet Letter,* as seen and pondered by Tony Soprano at Bowdoin College in "College," *The Sopranos,* season 1, episode 5.

Persona, in terms of origins, in and of itself implies performance and display. Jung, for instance, calls persona a mask, where one is "acting a role" (Jung et al. 1966, 167), whereas Goffman (1973) considers that performance and roles are at the center of everyday life and everyday forms and patterns of communication.

In recent work, I have used persona to describe how online culture pushes most people to construct a public identity that resembles what celebrities have had to construct for their livelihood for at least the last century (Marshall 2010a; 2014a). My work has expanded to an investigation of how online persona relates to individual agency (Marshall 2013) and professional postures and positioning (Barbour and Marshall 2012).

The fictive constructions, then, are intensified versions of what persona is addressing: the fabrication of a role for particular directions and ends. Characters or *personnages* are constructed personas for very directed ends. Their limitation to the study of persona as a dimension of public culture is that they are not real; however, when one thinks of the actor who takes on this fictive identity, there is clearly a relationship between the real personality and that of the character. Moreover, as Nayar's (2009) analysis of highly famous characters that are fictitious reveals, these celebrated characters, such as Harry Potter or Wolverine, sometimes take on a public presence in and of themselves. To capture this public movement of a fictional character, Nayar blends the term *celebrity* with *fiction* and calls these semipublic–semireal entities "celefiction": the characters are famous, are highly visible, and move across media, informational, and cultural platforms with ease and speed (18–20). Their celebrity status underlines their power to move outside of their primary text into public discourse and through public spaces—an extratextual movement that fundamentally defines what a celebrity embodies (Marshall [1997] 2014).

Seriality has to be seen as fundamental to a *personnage*'s power of and extension into the public world. For instance, with Harry Potter again, at least some of his recognition is dependent on the linking or seriating of the related books and movies. Seriality helps organize our sense of affective connection to our popular culture. The familiarity of some element of repetition is both comforting for audiences and provides at least a sense of guarantee or warranty that they will enjoy the future text as much as they enjoyed the past related text. Seriality, though, also produces myriad other effects and affects that provide a useful background for understanding its utility in both the understanding of character and its value in investigating contemporary public persona.

Etymologically, the words *series* and *seriality* are from the Latin and refer to "succession" in classical usage, and they are identified with ancestry and the patterns of identification and linking descendants. The original use of *seriality* highlights its value in understanding the formation of the constitution of person and persona and how the past and ancestry connect in series to the current or contemporary self. Its current usage, however, has broadened metaphorically outward to identify anything that is in sequence or linked or joined: it can be a series of lectures and arguments or a related mark of cars manufactured in manners that are stylistically linked. It has since been deployed to capture the production process of various cultural forms, and one of the key origins of this usage came from the nineteenth-century novel.

Examples of where the nineteenth-century novel was sold and presented in serial form are too numerous even to summarize here. It is useful to use Dickens's serial production as a defining example of how seriality moved into popular culture and the entertainment industry more broadly. Part of the reason for the sheer length of many of Charles Dickens's works is their original distribution as serials. In fact, all his novels were first distributed in chapters in monthly form in magazines or newspapers. A number of related consequences from Dickens's serialization are relevant to understanding seriality in entertainment culture more widely (Hayward 1997). First, his novel serialization established a continuous connection to his readers over years. Thus Dickens's name itself became synonymous with and connected to an international reading public. Second, his use of seriality established a production form that was seen to be more affordable to its audience: seriality has to be understood as a form that is closely connected to economies and markets as cultural commodities kneaded their way into the structure of everyday life. And third, seriality established through repetition not only the author's name but the names of the key characters that populated the cultural form. Although not wholly attributable to the serial nature of the delivery, characters such as Oliver Twist, Ebenezer Scrooge, and David Copperfield, along with a host of other major and minor players in his many books, become integrated into everyday discourse because of their ever-present and delayed delivery over stories over time (see Allen 1985, 78–79). In the same way that newspapers became part of the vernacular of contemporary culture, fictional characters from novels lived for years at a time in the consciousness of this large reading public. The characters or *personnages* themselves became personalities that, through usage, became a way of describing other behaviors. One can think of Uriah Heep and his sheer obsequiousness in *David Copperfield* as a character type that became part of popular culture thinking, expressing a clear negative sentiment about a personality trait.

In the twentieth century, serials became associated much more with book series. One of the more successful serial genres was the murder mystery. It developed what could be described as recognizable *personnages* that were both fictional and real. Thus the real Agatha Christie, with her consistent and prodigious production of short whodunit novels, was linked to her Belgian fictional detective Hercule Poirot. Variations of these serial constructions occurred in children's fiction, the emerging science fiction genre, and westerns, with authors and characters rising to related prominence.

In a similar vein, early- to mid-twentieth-century film produced the film serial. In its production and exhibition, the film serial was a déclassé genre in its overt emphasis on the economic quality of seriality. Thus the film serial was generally a filler genre that was interspersed before and after a feature film at screenings (Dixon 2011). As well as producing a familiarity with characters such as Flash Gordon, it was also instrumental in producing actors with a public profile that grew from this repetition. Flash Gordon was not just a character; he was also the actor Buster Crabbe, and over time, the association became indissoluble for audiences and actor alike. Feature film serials also developed in the first half-century of American cinema in particular, with child actors like Shirley Temple, Mickey Rooney, and Judy Garland often reprising variations of their previous roles.

Seriality has more or less become the standard form of delivery of broadcast media for most of the last seventy years, and this has been driven by the economies of production it developed. Whether the production was news, comedy, or drama, most radio and television forms were and are variations of serials. As well as being the zenith of seriality, television serials have been the most studied form of seriality of all cultural forms and are thus the greatest source of research into what serials actually produced. The classic serial that began on radio and migrated to television was the soap opera. Although most of the long-running soap operas have now disappeared, many have endured for more than thirty years, with the American series *The Guiding Light* lasting seventy-two years and the British soap *Coronation Street* now in its sixty-fourth year. Australian nighttime soap operas have managed a similar longevity: *Neighbours* is in its thirtieth year, while *Home and Away* is in its twenty-seventh year. Many of the analyses of soap operas and serials deal with the narrative and the potential long narrative arcs related to characters and story lines. In contrast to most evening television serials historically, soap operas maintain the continuity from one episode to the next in an unbroken narrative. Evening television serials, such as situation comedies, though maintaining long arcs over their run, are episodic in nature: the structure of the story is generally concluded in the given episode with at least partial closure in a manner that is never engaged in the never-ending soap opera serials.

Although other cultural forms deploy seriality in their structures—one can think of comic books and manga as two other obviously connected and highly visible serial sources—online and video games represent the other key media platform of serials in contemporary culture. Once again, a "horizon of expectation" (Jauss and De Man 1982, 23) motivates the iteration of new versions of games by the industry. New versions of games are designed to build on gamer loyalties while augmenting the quality and possibilities of the particular game. Game culture and gamers have a different structural relationship to serials, which at least Denson and Jahn-Sudmann (2013) describe as digital seriality: a new version of a game is also imagined to be technologically more sophisticated in its production value, and this transformation of the similitude of game structure with innovation drives the economy of what are often described as "franchises." New versions of Minecraft or Call of Duty draw the literal reinvestment of the gamer. New consoles provide a further push to serialization of games as they accentuate some transformed quality in gameplay, interaction, or quality of animated graphics. Sports franchises are perhaps the most serialized form of game: to replicate new professional seasons in each major sport, the sports game transforms with a new coterie of players each year.

From these various venues, one can see the centrality of seriality in cultural forms. There is no question that one of the dimensions of seriality that transcends these cultural forms is its coordination and intersection with the development of the industrialization of culture, and this understanding of the economic motivation behind series has been explored in some of the earliest analyses of seriality (see Hagedorn 1988; Browne 1984). Also, seriality has been mined extensively in terms of its production of the pleasure of repetition and transformation. Whether in studies of readers of romance fiction (Radway 1984) or fans of science fiction television (Tulloch and Jenkins 1995; Jenkins 1992), serials have provided the resource for exploring the power of the audience to connect, engage, and reconstruct texts.

The serialization of character—the production of a public *personnage*—and its relation to persona surprisingly has been understudied. Though certain writers have remarked on the longevity of a certain character, such as Vicky Lord's forty-year character on the soap opera *One Life to Live,* and the interesting capacity to maintain both complicated and hidden story lines (de Kosnik 2013), and though fan audience studies have looked at the parasocial–familiar relationship that fan and character construct, less has been developed about the relationship of the serial character, the actor, and a form of twinned public identity. Seriality does produce a patterning of *personnage,* a structure of familiarity for the audience, but also a structure of performance for the actor. For instance, in a longitudinal analysis of the character of Fu Manchu, Mayer (2012) is able to discern how a patterning of iconic form shapes, replicates, and reiterates the look of Fu Manchu across decades of films. Similarly, there has been a certain work on the "taxonomy of character" where the serial character of a television program is analyzed in terms of six parts: physical traits and appearance, speech patterns, psychological traits and habitual behaviors, interaction with other characters, environment, and biography (Pearson, as cited in Lotz 2013).

From seriality, what emerges is a particular kind of "typecasting" where the actor becomes wedded to the specific iteration of the taxonomy of performance. Like other elements related to seriality, serial character performance is also closely aligned to the economic. In previous writing, I have described this economic patterning of performance in chapter 2 as the John Wayne syndrome. Wayne's career developed into a form of serial performance where the individual born as Marion Morrison becomes structured into a cultural and economic category that determines the next film role. The economic weight of type also constructs the limits and range of the actor. Type or typage as a form of casting has always been an element of film and theatrical performance; but it is the seriality of performance—the actual construction of a *personnage* that flows between the fic-

John Wayne syndrome: the typecast.

tional and real person—that allows an actor to claim a persona that can be exchanged within the industry. Even fifteen years after his death, Wayne remained one of the most popular performers in the United States, his status unrivaled in its close definition of American value that became wedded with a conservative masculinity and politics (Wills 1997).

Type and typecasting have an interesting relationship to seriality. From Eisenstein's original use of the term *typage,* where the character is chosen to fit into the meaning of the film and the image was placed into its sequence to make that meaning, it generally describes the circumscribing of the actor into his look. As Wojcik's analysis reveals, typecasting in various periods of theater and film acting has been seen as something to be fought for by actors (in the 1850s) and actively resisted in Hollywood in 1950 by the Screen Actors Guild in support of a greater range of roles for each actor. It is also seen as something that leads to cultural stereotypes that can reinforce the racial profiling that has haunted diverse cultures and the dangers of law enforcement for centuries (Wojcik 2004, 169–71). Early writers in the study of film acting emphasized that its difference from theater was that in film, the actor and character converged in terms of connected reality and a physicality: the film actor was less a mask and more a sense of "being" (Kracauer [1960] 2004). Cavell's ([1979] 2004, 34) work suggested film over stage performance allowed an individuality over type to emerge. Thompson's ([1978] 2004) semiotic "commutation" test was another way of assessing the power of the individual "star" actor to be seen as elemental to the construction and meaning of the film role. Television produced with regularity character actors, where performance and identity became indissoluble partly because of the sheer repetition and the massive visibility of these seriated performances.

The overdetermined Nimoy as Spock: inescapable.

One of the most typecast individuals in television history was Leonard Nimoy as Spock in *Star Trek*: although the original *Star Trek* series ran for only three seasons, the physical caricature of Spock in the series as half-Vulcan, half-human made it difficult for the actor Nimoy to exit the role (Laws 2013). Indeed, his famous autobiography riffed on this misidentity with the forceful but still economically powerful title *I Am Not Spock* in 1975. When Nimoy perceived that his fans thought that he was unhappy in his role as Spock, he published a further tome, *I Am Spock,* that righted his relationship to his fictional identity and its continued source of roles for the previous thirty years (Nimoy 1995). Although it is usually perceived as quite different in its constitution of a public identity, a very similar structure of persona developed around the American CBS news anchor Walter Cronkite. With his status as anchor confirmed in its power and centrality to American culture in his desk reportage of the assassination and death of President Kennedy in November 1963, Cronkite went on to inhabit a persona as the most trusted man in the United States by the sheer gravitas of hosting the *Evening News* stripped across every weeknight at 6:30 P.M. for the next nineteen years. In contrast to Nimoy, Cronkite *became* Cronkite the television news anchor, where persona, actor, and professional identity merged—at least in terms of almost all forms of the man's visibility.

From this vantage point of understanding the seriality of character/*personnage* and how it informs the idea of the actor, I want to provide a longer conclusion about how seriality informs the concept of persona in the contemporary moment. First of all, what this study reveals is the way in which the production of identity is overlaid onto any conception of identity itself. If we can understand persona not in any negative formulation but rather as a form of productive performance of a public self, then it becomes very useful to see that these very visible public blendings of performance and the actor-self can make sense more generally as to how the public self is produced and constituted. My final and concluding examples will try to elucidate this insight further.

In 2013, Netflix launched into the production of original drama with its release of *House of Cards.* The series itself was remarkable for a number of reasons. First among them, it was positioned as a quality series and clearly connected to the lineage of recent American subscription television programs such as *The Sopranos, Six Feet Under, Dexter, Mad Men, The Wire, Deadwood,* and *True Blood,* among a few others. *House of Cards* was an Americanized version of a celebrated British miniseries. In the American version, an ambitious party whip, Frank Underwood, maneuvers with ruthlessness and the calculating support of his wife closer to the presidency and the heart and soul of American power. How the series expressed quality was at least partially in its choice of actors. The role of Frank Underwood was played by the respected film actor Kevin Spacey. His wife, Claire, was played by the equally high-profile Robin Wright.

Frank and Clare Underwood: the power of persona in acting and career.

Quality was also expressed through the connection of the audience of viewers to an antihero: a *personnage* that was not filled with virtue but moved with Machiavellian acuity toward his objective of ultimate power. This idea of quality emerged in many ways from the successful construction of the character of Tony Soprano by James Gandolfini in the acclaimed HBO television series *The Sopranos,* which reconstructed the very conception of the family in organized crime. Tony Soprano was enacted as complex and conflicted, with a sense of right and justice, but embedded in the *personnage* were psychological tropes and scars and an understanding of the need for violence to maintain influence power and a perverse but natural sense of order (Martin 2013).

The new television serial character now embodied a larger code and coterie of acting: from *The Sopranos,* there is the underlying sense and sensibility of method acting (see Vineberg 1991; Stanislavski [1961] 1989). Gandolfini inhabited the role of

Tony Soprano and used inner and hidden drives and motivations to become the source for the display of the character. Likewise, Spacey inhabits Frank Underwood. In that new habitus of television character, the actor becomes subsumed by the role. Gandolfini becomes overdetermined by the role and his own identity as an actor becomes melded to the role. Kevin Spacey, despite his longer and highly visible history as a film actor, is overwhelmed by the televisual role of Frank Underwood. Its serial power, where audiences connect for hours and hours, where the actor commits to weeks and weeks of shoots, and years and years of being the character—a serious character with emotional depth, with psychological motivation that rivals the most visceral of film roles—transforms the actor into a blended public person and the related *personnage*.

This blend of fictional and public life is complex as much for the producing actor as it is for the audience that makes the habitus real. What Kevin Spacey/Frank Underwood inhabit is a blended persona, whose power is dependent on the constructed identity that is at source the actor's production as much as any institutional form or any writer or director connected to making *House of Cards* "real." There is no question that this serial public identity will be difficult for Kevin Spacey to disentangle when the series ends; in many ways it will be an elemental part of his continuing public identity. This is the economic power and risk of seriality.

One can see similar blendings in the persona in popular music and its own form of contemporary seriality in performance. For example, Eminem is a stage name for a person sometimes called Marshall Mathers; but Eminem takes this a step further and produces beyond a character in its integration of the personal—a real *personnage,* Slim Shady, to inhabit his music and its stories. To further complexify this construction, Eminem relies on the production of his stories with elements that appear to be from his everyday life (Dawkins 2010). His characterizations, because of the emotional depth he inhabits through his rapped stories,

Eminem: Marshall Mathers: Slim Shady.

betray a connection to his own psychological state. Following in the history of popular music performance where the singer-songwriter's work is seen by all to present a version of the public self that is closer emotionally to the private self, we once again see how the seriality of performance begins to produce a blended public persona. Rap music has inherited this seriality of produced identity from twentieth-century icons of the singer-songwriter and its display of the public–private self—in reverse order, from grunge to punk, from folk to blues.

Finally, it is worthwhile to think of online culture in similar ways in the production of public personas. Seriality is elemental to online culture. Social media encourage the production of public identities through forms of repetition of that identity. To establish a public profile, social media users establish an identity with some consistency over time. The everydayness in the production of the public self online thus resembles the production and performance of seriality in fiction. Professional social media sites such as LinkedIn encourage the consistency of public identity, and this is very important in understanding the new versions of the public self that are deployed in contemporary culture. However, much like the new psychological depth that is part of the meaning of serial characters such as Frank Underwood in *House of Cards,* Slim Shady for Eminem, or Tony Soprano in *The Sopranos,* social media seriality also encourages greater revelations of the private self via Instagram and Facebook walls and images. We are collectively reconstituted as personas online, seriated by the continuing presence of our online sites and regularly drawn to reveal more and greater depths of our character. In other words, the online persona resembles the new depth of the quality television serial *personnage* with elaborate arcs and great complexity. Seriality in our public identity is also uncovered in the production of our game avatars, where, to develop trust and connection with friends in online settings, we maintain our identity and our patterns of gameplay. At the core of this online identity is a desire for visibility, and we are drawn to be "picked up" and shared in some repeatable form across what we each perceive as a meaningful dimension of culture. Through the circulation of viral images, texts, and videos, we engage in a circulation and repetition of meaning that feeds back into the constancy and value of an online identity. Through memes, we replicate and seriate content that at some level seriates personas in terms of humor, connection, and value.

Seriality is central to understanding the formation of our masks of public identity and is at least one valuable analytical way to understand the development of the contemporary persona. This essay represents the first foray into thinking through the relationship between seriality and persona.

9. Intercommunication and Cultures of Surveillance

Introduction: Utopian and Dystopian Technological Formations of Change

For the last century, different authors have tried to argue that technology is fundamentally changing who we are and what we do. These notions of the future have been on a spectrum from utopian to dystopian. For instance, Teilhard de Chardin's "noosphere" and Omega Point identify the idea of a networked and autonomous organism emerging from our connections (Steinhart 2008). In some ways, the noosphere resembles Pierre Lévy's (1997) claim that contemporary technology has spawned a kind of "collective intelligence," and most of his subsequent work has been an analysis of this emerging phenomenon. Alvin Toffler's (1971) best-selling *Future Shock* similarly identifies the juggernaut of technological change and how we must adapt to it for our own survival. Langdon Winner's (1977) early work on "autonomous technology" helps explain this predilection and the sometimes fear with which we approach technology: increasingly, technology is conceptualized as working without supervision in a manner that is beyond automatic—what Victor Ferkiss (1969) identified and Winner (1977) concurred as "technics out of control."

The development of the Internet for more than thirty years, and particularly the Web for the last twenty years, has served as a new site for the speculation around technological change. In many ways, the debates echo and resonate with some of these past considerations of technology. In fact, a component of media and communication studies, led by Levinson (1999), buttressed by *Wired* magazine, and expanded by the Toronto Media lab, has resurrected McLuhan and proclaimed that many of his insights around media and the exteriorization of the senses now make sense in the networked era of the Internet. In related parallel veins, others, such as Jenkins and his notion of participatory media being made possible through new media forms and their facilities of connecting, sharing, and producing, have taken the insights from cultural studies and repainted them into a study of both "transmedia" and networked "fandom" as an effective model to describe the uses made of contemporary culture (see Jenkins 2006a; 2006b; Jenkins, Ford, and Green 2013). Axel Bruns (2008), in developing and deploying the term *produsage* to describe online experience, where the individual is no longer an audience member but a hybrid of producer and user that is engaged in her media consumption/production, has advanced that an identifiable public sphere—nuanced through his study of Twitter as micro-, meso-, and macroforms of communication—is developing through the hundreds of millions who are now using social media platforms such as Twitter and Facebook (Bruns and Moe 2014, 15–28). Social thinkers, such as Harrison Rainie and Barry Wellman (2012), have taken their analysis of the online networked life and celebrated the powers and communities produced through the new networked individualism.

In contrast, the dystopian critiques of the Internet and new technologies of communication and information have revolved around one principal theme: that the technologies we have most embraced have allowed the expansion of a culture of surveillance. Although there are many variations on this critique of technology, one of the most interesting is related to how online entities gather personal information about us, aggregate it, and send it on to interested parties, such as advertisers (see Turow 2011). A variation of this critique is related to privacy and how the new movement of information online has allowed for all sorts "erosions of privacy" (Rule 2007) and even identity theft. In addition to this form of surveillance and threats to privacy, there is a general belief post–Snowden crisis that governments are likewise compiling and aggregating information about individuals as they search for forming moments of illegality and potential terrorism (Ball and Wood 2013).

Technology's Effect on Subjectivity: The Transformed Self

The argument that follows is an analysis of how these technological pushes identify a change in subjectivity in contemporary culture. The utopian and dystopian discourses around technology isolate an apparent cultural change and point to elements of exhilarating empowerment and its dialectic, the sense of powerlessness and manipulation. These polar opposites actually have led to an easy game of critique and countercritique, with accusations of technological determinism floating close to the surface of most of these analyses. What I would like to pursue here is how these elements are producing a public self that resembles the citizen, the consumer, the audience member, and other categories of the public self—but are qualitatively different than these categories of the self. Central to this argument is understanding how this technocultural shift has produced a different relationship and organization of the self in terms of the public, the private, and the intimate. It has led to different strategies of the production of the self that are building in our culture as individuals work tactically and strategically in territories and on grounds that demand a different constitution of the self.

Understanding the Implications of "Intercommunication": Its Key Components

Conceptually, what is occurring is a distinctively transformed engagement with the public world. In previous work, I have developed the concept of *intercommunication* to help describe this new configuration that identifies a shift in the use of media and a different intersection in forms of personal communication that relate to media (Marshall 2010a; 2014a). One of the difficulties in both analyzing and describing what are now called either social networks or social media is that on the surface, they appear to be a form of mediated interpersonal communication. Once one begins looking more closely at the content that is prevalent on Facebook, Instagram, Twitter, Tumblr, and Pinterest, among many other forms of social networks that are used regularly by an estimated 73 percent of Americans, for example (Pew 2013), and by more than 1.4 billion people worldwide (Statistic Brain 2014), it becomes evident that the interpersonal operates as a sophisticated filter of all sorts of messages that come from a variety of sources. Thus media sources are highly prevalent on Facebook walls and are interspersed with very personal photos and commentaries for the vast majority of users. Music is regularly shared, liked, and commented on. YouTube videos, a partial social network in and of itself, with its channels and commentary, are linked via social media, leading to a dissemination and, ultimately, an exhibition of amateur and professional content. Media and entertainment images and articles are commonly part of Facebook users' communication platform. Social media, then, are a varied combination of interpersonal communication and highly mediated forms of communication. What has been naturalized is the individual as the fiber that connects these formerly distinct worlds together. As an application of technology, social networks produce several kinds of social patterns that are fundamentally defined as communication, and because of this integrated nature, they are best described as "intercommunication." The fundamental components of intercommunication are listed and described as follows. These components of intercommunication are a means of synthesizing the way online culture has worked to shape contemporary subjectivity:

Individualized. Although not completely, the economics of the current generation of the online economy are organized around the individual. Our social media accounts are personal and are connected to equally individualized e-mail accounts. Even the structure of identifying our "homes" on social media is dependent on this form of individual registration, which transforms the most institutional corporation or organization into an individual profile. This individualization is a form of online affordance, as its structure naturally fits into the individual structures of payments, accounts, and credit that predated the Internet in banking. The individualized structure of online culture facilitates the related relationship to personal security and has led to the prevalent discourse around protection and privacy that circulates around the economic self whether online or offline. It also has intersected with how new economies develop online. The purchase of "applications" or "apps" became a new business structure with the development of the Apple smartphone as individuals were invited to expand the functions on their devices through downloading the software or online platform onto their mobile phones (Goggin 2011). Whether free or for a charge, the application dimension of the online economy demanded an individualized structure of registration that once again facilitated a banking-like identity.

Interpersonal. The attractiveness of the contemporary Web, from Web 2.0 to what is called now more ominously the Semantic Web (a term originally coined by Tim Berners-Lee and now used to differentiate the power of the Web to make sense of and relate data and produce new information for those who have control of those data), has generally been linked to its capacity to make connections to one's friends. Facebook privileges the notion of friends, while Twitter's relations are determined by a much more prophet-like terminology of followers. In both cases, social media have made online communication less formal than letter writing or its more modern variation, e-mail. Twitter's 140-character limitation has privileged aphoristic forms of communication that imply an interpersonal understanding—in many cases—even to be understood. Threads of communication on Facebook or via Twitter are comfortably written in half-sentences or caption-like as they connect to associated images and resemble text messaging. This value of the interpersonal is privileged in using social media. Prestige is at least partially bestowed by the numbers of friends and followers one has in the system. More importantly, the interpersonal connection defines the valuation of social media over other forms of media: the actions of "sharing" and of "liking," the related actions of "retweeting" or "starring," are the engines of the online economy. The movement of this kind of shared information defines relative interest as well as the points where individuals are interpersonally aggregated. What is attractive to the user—the capacity to connect to and share with friends—is also the exact location where monetizing begins by the social network companies.

Indexical. If sharing and exchanging are the key experiential elements of social media experience and define its qualities of intercommunication, they also underline the value of what can be described as indexical forms of communication. From semiotics, an indexical sign is one that points to or implies a relationship to another sign (see Chandler 2007, 37, 42–44). Indexical communication defines the constant effort to extend communication from one image, text, or video to another. The indexical quality of intercommunication via social media identifies the way in which the various forms of advertising and cultural industries work to insinuate themselves into the personal construction of value that social media produces. The indexical dimensions further highlight the way in which communication is extended and augmented in online culture.

Multiple registers of communication. From the term itself, intercommunication implies that different registers of communication are visible and invested in simultaneously. Thus chat is linked with images; a YouTube video may construct a broadcast form of address in its parasocial relationship to its audience, but when it is repositioned into an interpersonal form of exchange, this style of communication is altered. This multiregistered structure of communication that intercommunication expresses is perhaps best seen in meme culture. A particular video or image is transformed by users for its rearticulation and reexpression across online culture. The universe of a particular meme may include millions, but its rearticulation may be designed for just a few hundred friends (see Shifman 2013). These multiple registers imply formal, informal, personal, and intimate forms of communication that are all connected to the same Facebook account.

Internetworked. The individual of online culture is constantly aggregated. In the first order, as I have discussed under the category of the interpersonal, we as users of social media are encouraged to connect and make connections. Game players are rewarded for their ability to develop friendship networks in different online settings. The significance of connection is twofold. For the individual, it defines a different constitution of value and identity. Connections determine reputation as they work to configure the presentation of the self to a defined micropublic world. For the industry, networks and connections are the means to establish economic value. The interrelated quality of identity online allows different kinds of information to be generated as well as providing the source for greater and greater exchanged content. The actual information contained in the shared content helps define our identities further, and this information has become the economic fuel of the Semantic Web: although information appears to define the social and reputational dimensions of the user, it also regularly defines how that identity intersects with commodities and services. For example, if our interpersonal communication consistently addresses personal fitness and exercise, it is very likely that the intercommunication environment that the individual inhabits online will have links, images, and connections to fitness applications for tablets and iPhones or diet and exercise advice and products. The internetworked movement of information of the self actually generates personalized content that in its direct address plays with older media's more removed form and register of advertising address.

Intercommunicative Public Persona:
Online Culture's Transformation of the Public Self

It is a significant question to explore our awareness as users of how online culture and its pervasive use is transforming our notion of ourselves. Intercommunication has certainly become naturalized through our use of social networks and mobile media in our everyday practices. The level of that naturalization defines how much we have integrated the new dimension of a kind of public display of the self. Nonetheless, online culture—as evidenced through the billions using social media and the Internet as part of their daily lives—does make us sensitive to a new version of ourselves, a persona, that is formed through what we do and present online. Living and experiencing intercommunication makes that persona related to the values promulgated through these online locations. A patterning of a public self is emerging from this intercommunicative environment. It is a strategic and pragmatic persona—a mask that should be seen not necessarily as a negation of a truer self but rather as a technique to move through a transformed public world. What follows is an application of these components of intercommunication and how they have begun to structure individual variations of an *intercommunicative public persona.*

Specular Persona: The Particular Specular Quality of Contemporary Culture

One element of online culture and the related social media is that the individual leaves consistent traces of identity. These traces go well beyond filling out profile pages and registering accounts. Facebook in particular has trails of images and comments, updates and responses. The intercommunicative environment means that an archive of the self's forms of communication remains as a sediment over time. Unlike verbal communication, which is temporally evanescent, however much our memory attempts to reconstruct it, social network account-homes structure a highly developed version of ourselves over time—a timeline of engagement, investment, and exchange. No matter how much we imagine that social networks are about connection, they also make us look at ourselves and how we present ourselves to the world every time we sign on and check in. This public dimension of the timeline of media and communication pushes us to read ourselves as others might read us (see Rosenberg and Egbert 2011). In other words, our Facebook homepage becomes a mirror of our public identity, and we use our sites to preen, to adjust, and to edit ourselves. Our homepages makes us internalize the processes of how we present ourselves through this particular presentational media.

Serial Persona: Archiving the Self/Managing the Self

Simultaneously, our sites on LinkedIn or Facebook or Instagram begin also to archive our identity. The recent tenth-anniversary video produced by Facebook for each of its users underlines the way in which we are mediatized in our construction of our public online identity and its relationship to time (see Brady 2014). These archives work in different temporal loops. We

expose versions and variations of our identity poses that produce daily forms of interaction with our friends and followers:
in this way the temporal loop has the currency of news media.
Our status updates provide the immediacy and presence of our
personas. A longer temporal loop is collected through what
we store on our social media sites and also how we categorize
those forms of storage. Thus photos may be collected over time
and grouped under trips, events, and people. Our longer temporal identity is determined by text and image conversations
that establish how we project our own form of networked self.
The replies of others and our own replies to others determine
a kind of internal ranking of value. Through our links to our
favorite forms of media, images and videos are pushed our way
in news feeds or on our walls based on our prior decisions as
to what we like. We allow these media favorites and their promotional feeds and content to define us in some parasocial way
that makes us included and belonging in their core, faithful and
fanlike audience.

It is difficult to describe effectively the archived self that
is part of how we manage this intercommunication. Besides
our direct accounts of social media, our online identities are
also shaped by what appears when our names are "searched"
through search engines like Google. In addition, our images are
sometimes "tagged" and thereby appear to our friends whenev-
er we make an appearance in a post. Because of this quality of
search in this online intercommunication environment, there
is an identity accumulation that becomes associated with our
online activities. The best way to describe this layered identity
is to link it with how television characters and the actors who
are associated with them take on a serialized drama. The online
persona is very much like this serialized character of ourselves:
it resembles us and, in some instances, is very close to our identity, but it remains something that is a projection of our self for

particular and directed purposes. It is essentially a serial persona derived from the archive of material that circulates around our online activity (see Marshall 2014a).

Reputational Persona: Status

Implied in both the ideas of the specular persona and of the serial persona is that this new intercommunication world also has expectations that we are managing our reputations in some way. The many moral panics around youth and online culture usually deal with issues of reputation management out of control: thus we hear of potential employers checking social media and searching online only to discover that a potential employee is revealed to have a drinking problem or other form of social or sexual indiscretion (Messieh 2012). Similarly, university admission officers are now known to survey social media when apparently equal applicants exceed places to differentiate candidates (Urist 2013). Scandals, which have been one of the tropes of celebrity discourse for most of the last century, are now seen to be the bête noire of online culture. The plenitude of images, comments, and connections to people who may no longer be "friends" presents the possibility that one's persona could be transformed and reconstructed. This transformation threat is not exactly identity theft in the classic notion of fraud, but it does describe how an intercommunication sensibility produces what can be described as an ascendant focus on a "reputational persona" (Madden and Smith 2010). With the flow of individualized information that is shared across social networks and divided and reaggregated through data analysis, a large element of online activity is shaping the constructed identity that has developed or is developing for the individual. Like celebrities themselves, individuals have to manage their level of online access to privacy and intimacy: on one hand, revealing the self connects you to others and in some ways provides the affective "flash" and "allure" that maintain your presence; on the other hand, constructing a professional identity or—without the burden of a work identity—a presentable identity becomes at least considered in the contemporary moment.

A reputational persona is focused on the management of status and connects to the instability of public identity that has been an elemental part of capitalist culture for the last two centuries (De Botton 2004). For some, the connection to as many others is of great significance, and one's reputation is determined not only by the number of friends and followers one brings together through an online persona but also by the power and influence of those friends. As Marwick's (2013) research on Silicon Valley culture illustrated, this idea of influence, power, and reputation was essential for many in their management of their technology-related careers. Individuals attempted to connect to new businesses as well as new ideas and trends in the development of online applications and companies through social media and online networked connections. In a similar vein, Klout, the online application that tries to calibrate influence, works to build the value of reputation for both itself and individuals and thereby works to monetize influence and brand the self (Hearn 2010; Hearn and Schoenhoff 2016). The reputational persona leads to a commodification of the self and what has come to be known in consumer studies literature as self-branding (Banet-Weiser 2012). Although managing a branded persona is ubiquitous, it is perhaps best seen in the individualized channels of YouTube. Reputation is determined by subscribers and viewers as the model of attention and reputation merge the old structure of broadcasting influence with the new, much more individualized invocations and connections of YouTube (see Burgess 2009).

Conclusion: A New Public–Private World

Contemporary identity is shaped by two dimensions that have emerged from technology and, specifically, the applied technology of this generation of online culture. The industry behind online culture cajoles, seduces, and invites the user to move into becoming part of a different public sphere. It is a public sphere defined not by citizenship but rather by participation and, maybe even more significantly, revelation. Whatever activity we engage in online, whether it be online gaming or social networking or watching, we are encouraged to participate in order to reveal elements of ourselves. This push to revelation has an economic motivation that we have detailed in this chapter as data about ourselves are collected by the companies that host our personal revelations for all sorts of purposes and ends. Equally, as online culture becomes more naturalized as part of everyday culture, with greater levels of participation in social media, gaming, and online viewing and reading, the production of an online self becomes normal and naturalized. As Rainie and Wellman (2012) detail, what is emerging is networked individualism: our awareness as individuals that we are part of elaborate and interconnected networks is another push toward the production of public versions of ourselves. The public persona produced in this environment of micropublics, rankings, and reputation is one that incorporates the exigencies of intercommunication. It pushes us toward what Jan-Hinrik Schmidt (2014) describes in his analysis of Twitter as "personal publics." Like Bentham's panopticon that Foucault (1995) detailed, we are aware, in our comportment of the public version of ourselves, of the way that intercommunication works. We are increasingly aware that we have to produce and present ourselves and that we have to work on this public self regularly and often.

This is a changed world that emerges from the application of technology and its reorganization of the value of the public presentation of the self. Increasingly, individuals in online culture are becoming pragmatic and strategic as they incorporate an intercommunication ethos into their online personas. Currently the personal and the private, and, for some, the intimate, are the engines of online culture; but perhaps we are moving toward a much more managed public persona. Hannah Arendt (1958) lamented that contemporary democracy has lost the divide and value between the public and the private. On first look, this new version of ourselves is incredibly revelatory and an extension of the intimate into the public sphere; but perhaps, like the panopticon, it is pushing us toward a new public sphere where all citizens are hyperaware of the public and private identities and separate them, where online culture becomes a very controlled public persona as we learn to develop and manage our public selves in an intercommunication environment.

Conclusion: Pandemic Persona

UNDERSTANDING PUBLIC IDENTITY is complex and certainly not homogeneous across the planet. It shifts in its value and its formation. As we have seen in our study of Stephen Colbert and Cate Blanchett, even relatively stable star personas are subject to strategic repositioning. The seriality of public identity is in constant negotiation and is dependent on past patterns and future desires. This series of excursions into exploring persona that this book has detailed has been structured to see the way in which it is not just a practice of the famous but an identity that all of us are forming and re-forming at some level. Although we imagine that Channing Tatum's life as a film star and former stripper is differently constituted (which has been oddly reconfigured through two of his films, *Magic Mike* [2012] and *Magic Mike XXL* [2015]), our contemporary moment allows us to form a variation of that persona through using glamour photography and all its accoutrements of star pampering and seductive and sexualized image making to temporarily inhabit that celebrated identity space.

The title of this Forerunner, *The Celebrity Persona Pandemic,* was chosen because it captured the contemporary condition in two significant ways. First of all, using the concept of persona to describe public identity is to emphasize its quality not as a true identity but as a fabricated and strategic presentation of the self (Marshall and Barbour 2015). Persona essentially means the self reconfigured for public display. In its public presentation, persona has to be understood as always in formation, always a type of performance and rendition of the self.

Second, persona is expanding as a practice in the contemporary moment. As detailed in chapter 11 in terms of the "intercommunicative self," the expansion of online culture has made it an expectation that we produce a persona for a variety of forms of social media. What is interesting about this process is that it is mediatized with its reconfiguration of the self through text, video, images, and a series of forms of exchange and intercourse with others that are at least partially automated (e.g., the simplified systems of "liking" someone else's posts provided by Facebook, Instagram, and Twitter). As my own research has explored, we are monitoring our selves for public consumption (Marshall and Barbour 2015) and exchange, and as much as we are looking at others, our culture has become quite specular (Marshall 2010b), in everyone's efforts at self-preening her own digital identity. In other words, we have entered an era when persona formation is central to the contemporary experience. Moreover, one can see that these pandemic practices of persona formation also necessitate greater and greater discussions of its value for our cultures and its repercussions across our constitution of identities. We need more research into the implications of how persona is changing and reconfiguring our cultures and our lives.

Through case studies and examples, *The Celebrity Persona Pandemic* has investigated this changed cultural condition, and through those examples, it has attempted to answer the core question of what form of value is emerging through the new and intensified focus on constructing a public self.

Assessing the value of something like persona is a tricky proposition. With the most famous, it is possible to break down the value of the celebrity persona into something economic and provide a monetary and notionally quantitative figure. Certainly the work of Currid-Halkett (2010, 23–45), where she identifies the "celebrity-residual," attempts to capture the sense that some public individuals possess something that transcends their primary activity and makes their very appearance valuable in and of itself. She makes the point that celebrity-residual is not a value that all well-known people have: for instance, in her reading, Bill Gates, the founder of Microsoft and the Gates Foundation, does not possess this extra "personal" dimension that we want to know more about as we would with someone like the actor Brad Pitt (30–31).

Other writers have also tried to investigate this world of the value of the public individual. Olivier Driessens (2013) uses the idea of "celebrity capital" to capture the way that celebrities' value via media moves across different fields and therefore presents the possibility of convertible value. Van Krieken (2012) identifies that celebrities are a kind of "attention" capital," a technique to draw audiences and their eyes. In a more scandalous style, Jo Piazza (2011) describes in detail how celebrities are used—and paid—to create events, sell magazines, and construct our world of entertainment value. The most comprehensive study of celebrity as a value is by Barry Gunter (2014), where in succeeding chapters, he works through how celebrity moves through these other dimensions of society and culture—from politics to consumer culture, from the corporate world to the psychological and health effects of celebrity activity and engagement. Gunter effectively maps why the endorsement by celebrities in all sorts of domains of contemporary life is so powerful and engaging.

The work of these various writers is important to understanding this public persona value, but it doesn't quite capture the way that persona is enacted more broadly than celebrity culture. To understand this extensive deployment of persona from the most famous to what might be called the everyday individual, it is perhaps useful to translate the nebulous and variable quality of value into something that can be seen as a potential form of power and influence.

The concept of *agency* comes closest to understanding the way that potential power across our globe in varied cultures is expressed through persona. First of all, our national and transnational celebrity cultures express a totemic caricature of our world and its organization of power: individual celebrities, such as Bono and his consumer/corporate-invested Red campaign, which provides funds to combat AIDS in Africa, or Angelina Jolie, whose concerted efforts at heralding the health value of her recent preemptive mastectomy derived from genetic knowledge, present clear evidence of agency. They are actors and agents in this highly privatized and individualized world who can effect change (see Marshall and Barbour 2015).

This level of agency is certainly not the same for the individual who is building an Instagram following via images of his cats in countless poses, or maybe another individual who is actively invested in a YouTube channel about how she plays her video games or repairs household fixtures. Nonetheless, whether we are looking at the agency of celebrities or the agency of active online individuals, they are working at making themselves visible in this privatized world.

The development, cultivation, distribution, and exhibition of a persona is now a normalized component of everyday life. The origins of its agency are embedded in the now centuries-old consumer culture where meaning and value are at least partially determined by the way that we display ourselves with and through the products we buy. Indeed, the advertising industry has cultivated the idea of agency embedded in every purchase of a shirt, every car we choose to buy, and every pair of shoes we choose to wear. In a manner similar to the way that Dick Hebdige (1979), among others, described spectacular youth subcultures more than thirty-five years ago and the subcultures' members' appropriation and revitalization of found consumer materials for their own negotiated, very public presentations of meaning, persona identifies the very public display of the self from the available materials of our now contemporary and increasingly online culture.

Producing and exhibiting a persona is not necessarily agency but at minimum a will-to-agency. It identifies that forms of attention—particularly online attention—are now very significant for both work and leisure. Persona, then, is the agent that produces value in all sorts of ways. First, it is the connecting glue that defines the organization of social media platforms, from Facebook and Twitter to Instagram and YouTube, by constructing friends and followers. Second, it publicizes our own likes and dislikes, our own patterns of attention, and shares these patterns with others. And third, persona allows for the collection of our information and identifies the real motor of the information economy as our self-generated information becomes the powerful and smart way our new consumer culture operates and thrives.

Given that persona is a construction of the self and a strategic entity for public use and is then recombined and recirculated through the engines and algorithms of the information economy, it may be useful in this conclusion to link its agency to how Bruno Latour has characterized agency. Latour (2007, 9) has developed through Actor Network Theory a different idea of agency: it is relational and associational and most provocatively identifies objects as actors and agents. Persona, in its construction and dissemination, is a characterization of the person, but it is essentially a formation of the self for particular purposes. It becomes the object for new associations in its genuine generation of information that is marked and shared as personal and deployed for all sorts of other activities and movement of data and information. As a new object, or at least a transformed object, in the contemporary world, it now redefines and restructures the way collectives are formed and operate. Persona is perhaps one of the essential ways for us to make sense of our world.

This book has been designed to show us how that this new form of agency is developing, transforming, and shifting the way our various cultures now operate. I hope its range of analyses of the formations of persona from the most celebrated to the most ordinary will at the very least stimulate others to investigate persona further.

References

Allen, Robert C. 1985. *Speaking of Soap Operas*. Chapel Hill: University of North Carolina Press.

Arendt, Hannah. 1958. *The Human Condition*. Charles R. Walgreen Foundation Lectures. Chicago: University of Chicago Press.

Ball, Kirstie S., and M. K. Wood. 2013. "Political Economies of Surveillance." *Surveillance and Society* 11, no. 1/2: 1–3.

Banet-Weiser, Sarah. 2012. *Authentic™: The Politics and Ambivalence in a Brand Culture*. Critical Cultural Communication. New York: New York University Press.

Barbour, K., and D. Marshall. 2012. "The Academic Online: Constructing Persona through the World Wide Web." *First Monday* 17, no. 9. http://firstmonday.org/htbin/cgiwrap/bin/ojs/index.php/fm/article/viewArticle/3969/3292.

boyd, danah. 2011. "Social Network Sites as Networked Publics." In *A Networked Self*, ed. Z. Papacharissi, 38–59. New York: Routledge.

———. 2014. *It's Complicated: The Social Lives of Networked Teens*. New Haven, Conn.: Yale University Press.

Browne, Nick. 1984. "The Political Economy of the (Super)Text." *Quarterly Review of Film Studies* 9, no. 3: 174–82.

Bruns, Axel. 2008. *Blogs, Wikipedia, Second life, and Beyond: From Production to Produsage*. Digital Formations. New York: Peter Lang.

Bruns, Axel, and Moe Hallvord. 2014. "The Structural Forms of Communications on Twitter." In *Twitter and Society*, ed. Katrin Weller, Axel Bruns, Jean Burgess, Merja Mahrt, and Cornelius Puschmann, 16–27. New York: Peter Lang.

Burgess, Jean. 2009. *YouTube: Online Video and Participatory Culture*. Digital Media and Society Series. Cambridge: Polity.

Cavell, Stanley. (1979) 2004. "Reflections on the Ontology of Film." In
    Movie Acting: The Film Reader, ed. Pamela Robertson Wojcik, 29–
    35. London: Routledge.

Chandler, Daniel. 2007. *Semiotics: The Basics.* Hoboken, N.J.: Taylor
    and Francis.

Checefsky, Bruce. 2008. "Photography and Desire: Fashion,
    Glamour and Pornography." In *The Concise Focal Encyclopedia
    of Photography: From the First Photo on Paper to the Digital
    Revolution,* ed. Michael R. Peres, 84–93. Amsterdam: Elsevier/
    Focal Press.

Currid-Halkett, Elizabeth. 2010. *Starstruck: The Business of Celebrity.*
    1st ed. New York: Faber and Faber.

Dawkins, Marcia Alesan. 2010. "Close to the Edge: Representational
    Tactics of Eminem." *Journal of Popular Culture* 43, no. 3: 463–85.

De Botton, Alain. 2004. *Status Anxiety.* New York: Pantheon Books.

de Kosnik, Abigail. 2013. "One Life to Live: Soap Opera Storytelling."
    In *How to Watch Television,* ed. Ethan Thompson and Jason
    Mittell, 355–63. New York: New York University Press.

Denson, Shane, and Andreas Jahn-Sudmann. 2013. "Digital Seriality:
    On the Serial Aesthetics and Practice of Digital Games." *Journal
    of Computer Game Culture* 7, no. 1: 1–32.

Dixon, Wheeler Winston. 2011. "Flash Gordon and the 1930s and
    40s Science Fiction Serial." *Screening the Past* 11. http://www
    .screeningthepast.com/2011/11/flash-gordon-and-the-1930s-and
    -40s-science-fiction-serial/.

Driessens, Olivier. 2013. "Celebrity Capital: Redefining Celebrity
    Using Field Theory." *Theory and Society* 42, no. 5: 543–60.

Dyhouse, Carol. 2010. *Glamour: Women, History, Feminism.* London:
    Zed Books.

Edwards, Louise P., and Elaine Jeffreys, eds. 2010. *Celebrity in China.*
    Hong Kong: Hong Kong University Press.

Ferkiss, Victor C. 1969. *Technological Man: The Myth and the Reality.*
    New York: New American Library.

Foucault, Michel. 1995. *Discipline and Punish: The Birth of the Prison.*
    New York: Vintage Books.

Giddens, A. 1991. *Modernity and Self-Identity: Self and Society in the
    Late Modern Age.* Cambridge: Polity.

Goffman, Erving. 1973. *The Presentation of Self in Everyday Life.*
    Woodstock, N.Y.: Overlook Press.

Goggin, Gerard. 2011. "Ubiquitous Apps: Politics of Openness in
    Global Mobile Cultures." *Digital Creativity* 22, no. 3: 148–59.

Gunter, Barrie. 2014. *Celebrity Capital: Assessing the Value of Fame*. New York: Bloomsbury.

Hagedorn, Roger. 1988. "Technology and Economic Exploitation: The Serial as a Form of Narrative Presentation." *Wide Angle* 10, no. 4: 4–12.

Harald, Christine. 2013. "'Brand You'!: The Business of Personal Branding and Communities in Anxious Times." In *The Routledge Companion to Advertising and Promotional Culture*, ed. M. P. McAllister and E. West, 341–56. New York: Routledge.

Hayward, Jennifer Poole. 1997. *Consuming Pleasures: Active Audiences and Serial Fictions from Dickens to Soap Opera*. Lexington: University Press of Kentucky.

Hazelkorn, E. 2011. *Rankings and the Reshaping of Higher Education: The Battle for World-Class Excellence*. Houndmills, U.K.: Palgrave Macmillan.

Hearn, Alison. 2010. "Structuring Feeling: Web 2.0, Online Ranking and Rating, and the Digital Reputation Economy." *Ephemera: Theory and Politics in Organization* 10, no. 3–: 421–38.

Hearn, Alison. 2013. "A Sentimental Greenbacks of Civilization: cartes de viste and the pre-history of self-branding." In *The Routledge Companion to Advertising and Promotional Culture*, ed. Matthew P. McAllister and Emily West, 24–38. New York: Routledge.

Hearn, Allison, and Stephanie Shoenhoff. 2016. "From Celebrity to Influencer: Tracing the Diffusion of Celebrity Value across the Data Stream." In *A Companion to Celebrity*, ed. P. David Marshall and Sean Redmond, 194–211. Boston: Wiley Blackwell.

Hebdige, Dick. 1979. *Subculture: The Meaning of Style*. London: Methuen.

Heinich, Nathalie. 2011. "Personne, personnage, personalité: L'acteur a l'ère de sa reproductibilité technique." In *Personne/personnage*, ed. Thierry Lenain and Aline Wiame, 77–101. Paris: Librairie Philosophique J. VRIN.

Hillis, K., Michael Petit, and Kylie Jarrett. 2013. *Google and the Culture of Search*. New York: Routledge.

Inglis, Fred. 2016. "The Moral Concept of Celebrity." In *A Companion to Celebrity*, ed. P. David Marshall and Sean Redmond, 21–38. Boston: John Wiley.

Jauss, Hans Robert, and Paul De Man. 1982. *Toward an Aesthetic of Reception*. Theory and History of Literature. Brighton, U.K.: Harvester.

Jenkins, Henry. 1992. *Textual Poachers: Television Fans and Participatory Culture*. Studies in Culture and Communication. New York: Routledge.

———. 2006a. *Convergence Culture: Where Old and New Media Collide.* New York: New York University Press.

———. 2006b. *Fans, Bloggers, and Gamers: Exploring Participatory Culture.* New York: New York University Press.

Jenkins, Henry, Sam Ford, and Joshua Green. 2013. *Spreadable Media: Creating Value and Meaning in a Networked Culture.* Postmillennial Pop. New York: New York University Press.

Jung, C. G., and C. G. Hull. 1966. *Two Essays on Analytical Psychology.* 2nd ed. Bollingen Series. Princeton, N.J.: Princeton University Press.

Kracauer, Siegfried. (1960) 2004. "Remarks on the Actor." In *Movie Acting: The Film Reader,* ed. Pamela Robertson Wojcik, 19–27. London: Routledge.

Latour, Bruno. 2007. *Reassembling the Social: An Introduction to Actor-Network-Theory.* Clarendon Lectures in Management Studies. Oxford: Oxford University Press.

Laws, Kevin. 2013. "Leonard Nimoy and Pharrell Williams: Star Trek and Creating Spock | Ep. 12 | Reserve Channel." https://www.youtube.com/watch?v=pYwk-ObP1Rw.

Lenain, Thierry, and Aline Wiame, eds. 2011. *Personne/personnage.* Paris: Librairie Philosophiques J. VRIN.

Levinson, Paul. 1999. *Digital McLuhan: A Guide to the Information Millennium.* New York: Routledge.

Lévy, Pierre. 1997. *Collective Intelligence: Mankind's Emerging World in Cyberspace.* New York: Plenum Trade.

Li, Hong-Mei. 2010. "From Chengfen to Shenjia: Granding and Promotional Culture in China." In *Blowing Up the Brand: Critical Perspectives on Promotional Culture,* ed. Melissa Aronczyk and Devon Powers, 145–69. Popular Culture and Everyday Life. New York: Peter Lang.

Lotz, Amanda D. 2013. "*House*: Narrative Complexity." In *How to Watch TV,* ed. Ethan Thompson and Jason Mittell, 22–29. New York: New York University Press.

Madden, M., and A. F. Smith. 2010. *Reputation Management and Social Media.* Washington, D.C.: Pew. http://www.pewinternet.org/2010/05/26/reputation-management-and-social-media/.

Maplesden, Alison. 2015. *Toxic Celebrity.* PhD diss., Deakin University.

Marshall, P. David. 1997. "The Commodity and the Internet: Interactivity and the Generation of the Audience Commodity." *Media International Australia,* February, 51–62.

——. (1997) 2014. *Celebrity and Power: Fame in Contemporary Culture.* 2nd ed. Minneapolis: University of Minnesota Press.

——. 2004. *New Media Cultures.* London: Oxford/Arnold.

——. 2010a. "The Promotion and Presentation of the Self: Celebrity as Marker of Presentational Media." *Celebrity Studies* 1, no. 1: 35–48. doi:10.1080/19392390903519057.

——. 2010b. "The Specular Economy: Celebrity, Two-Way Mirrors, and the Personalization of Renown." *Society* 47, no. 6: 498–502.

——. 2013. "Personifying Agency: The Public–Persona–Place–Issue Continuum." *Celebrity Studies* 4, no. 3: 369–71.

——. 2014a. "Persona Studies: Mapping the Proliferation of the Public Self." *Journalism* 15, no. 2: 153–70. doi:10.1177/1464884913488720.

——. 2014b. "Seriality and Persona." *M/C Journal* 17, no. 3. http://journal.media-culture.org.au/index.php/mcjournal/article/view/802.

——. 2015. "Monitoring Persona: Mediatized Identity and the Edited Public Self." *Frame: Journal of Literary Studies* 28, no. 1: 115–33.

——. 2016a. "Exposure: The Public Self Explored." In *A Companion to Celebrity,* ed. P. David Marshall and Sean Redmond, 497–517. Boston: Wiley Blackwell.

——. 2016b. "When the Private Becomes Public: Commodity Activism, Endorsement, and Making Meaning in a Privatized World." In *Contemporary Publics,* ed. P. David Marshall, Glenn D'Cruz, Sharyn McDonald, and Katja Lee, 229–46. New York: Palgrave Macmillan.

Marshall, P. David, and Kim Barbour. 2015. "Making Intellectual Room for Persona Studies." *Persona Studies* 1, no. 1: 1–12. https://ojs.deakin.edu.au/index.php/ps/article/view/464.

Martin, Brett. 2013. *Difficult Men: Behind the Scenes of a Creative Revolution—From "The Sopranos" and "The Wire" to "Mad Men" and "Breaking Bad."* London: Faber and Faber.

Marwick, Alice E. 2013. *Status Update: Celebrity, Publicity, and Branding in the Social Media Age.* New Haven, Conn.: Yale University Press.

——. 2016. "You May Know from YouTube: (Micro-)Celebrity in Social Media." In *A Companion to Celebrity,* ed. P. David Marshall and Sean Redmond, 194–211. Boston: Wiley Blackwell.

Mayer, R. 2012. "Image Power: Seriality, Iconicity, and the *Mask of Fu Manchu.*" *Screen* 53, no. 4: 398–417.

McGee, M. 2005. *Self-Help, Inc.: Makeover Culture in American Life.* Oxford: Oxford University Press.

Messieh, Nancy. 2012. "Survey: 37% of Your Prospective Employers Are Looking You Up on Facebook." *TNW,* April 18. http://thenextweb.com/socialmedia/2012/04/18/survey-37-of-your-prospective-employers-are-looking-you-up-on-facebook/.

Nayar, Pramod K. 2009. *Seeing Stars: Spectacle, Society, and Celebrity Culture.* New Delhi: Sage Publications.

Nelson, Chris. 2013. *Glamour Portrait.* Amherst Media.

Nimoy, Leonard. 1975. *I Am Not Spock.* Milbrae, Calif.: Celestial Arts.

——. 1995. *I Am Spock.* 1st ed. New York: Hyperion.

Pew Internet Research. 2013. "Social Networking Factsheet." September. http://www.pewinternet.org/fact-sheets/social-networking-fact-sheet/.

Piazza, Jo. 2011. *Celebrity, Inc.* Open Road/Integrated Media.

Radway, Janice A. 1984. *Reading the Romance: Women, Patriarchy, and Popular Literature.* Chapel Hill: University of North Carolina Press.

Rainie, Harrison, and Barry Wellman. 2012. *Networked: The New Social Operating System.* Cambridge, Mass.: MIT Press.

Raisborough, J. 2011. *Lifestyle Media and the Formation of the Self.* Houndmills, U.K.: Palgrave Macmillan.

Robards, Brady. 2014. "Digital Traces of the Persona through Ten Years of Facebook." *M/C Journal* 17, no. 3. http://journal.media-culture.org.au/index.php/mcjournal/article/view/818.

Rosenberg, Jenny, and Nichole Egbert. 2011. "Online Impression Management: Personality Traits and Concerns for Secondary Goals as Predictors of Self-Presentation Tactics on Facebook." *Journal of Computer-Mediated Communication* 17, no. 1: 1–18. doi:10.1111/j.1083--6101.2011.01560.x.

Rule, James B. 2007. *Privacy in Peril.* New York: Oxford University Press.

Samuels, John. 2015. "Stephen Colbert Chats with Two Gods on the Late Show." *CDA News.* October 3. https://cdanews.com/2015/10/stephen-colbert-chats-with-two-gods-on-the-late-show-video/.

Schmidt, Jan-Hinrik. 2014. "Twitter and the Rise of the Personal Publics." In *Twitter and Society,* ed. Katrin Weller, Axel Bruns, Jean Burgess, Merja Mahrt, and Cornelius Puschmann, 3–14. New York: Peter Lang.

Shifman, Limor. 2013. *Memes in Digital Culture.* Essential Knowledge Series. Cambridge, Mass.: MIT Press.

Stanislavski, Constantin. (1961) 1989. *Creating a Role.* New York: Routledge.

Statistic Brain. 2014. "Social Networking Statistics: 1.4 Billion Estimated Social Network Users." http://www.statisticbrain.com/social-networking-statistics/.

Steinhart, E. 2008. "Teilhard de Chardin and Transhumanism." *Journal of Evolution and Technology* 20, no. 1: 1–22.

Thompson, John O. (1978) 2004. "Screen Acting and the Commutation Test." In *Movie Acting: The Film Reader*, ed. Pamela Robertson Wojcik, 37–48. London: Routledge.

Toffler, Alvin. 1971. *Future Shock*. London: Pan.

Tulloch, John, and Henry Jenkins. 1995. *Science Fiction Audiences: Watching "Doctor Who" and "Star Trek."* Popular Fiction Series. London: Routledge.

Turow, Joseph. 2011. *The Daily You: How the New Advertising Industry Is Defining Your Identity and Your Worth*. New Haven, Conn.: Yale University Press.

Urist, Jacoba. 2013. "Application Angst: Teens' Social Media Can Hurt College Chances." *Today*, November 25. http://www.today.com /moms/application-angst-teens-social-media-could-hurt-college -chances-2D11641782.

Van Krieken, Robert. 2012. *Celebrity Society*. Hoboken, N.J.: Taylor and Francis.

Vineberg, Steve. 1991. *Method Actors: Three Generations of an American Acting Style*. New York: Schirmer Books.

Wills, Garry. 1997. *John Wayne's America: The Politics of Celebrity*. New York: Simon and Schuster.

Winner, Langdon. 1977. *Autonomous Technology: Technics-Out-of-Control as a Theme in Political Thought*. Cambridge, Mass.: MIT Press.

Wojcik, Pamela Robertson. 2004. "Typecasting." In *Movie Acting: The Film Reader*, ed. Pamela Robertson Wojcik, 169–89. London: Routledge.

P. David Marshall holds a personal chair in New Media, Communication, and Cultural Studies at Deakin University in Melbourne, Australia. He is also Distinguished Visiting Foreign Expert in the School of Journalism and Communication at Central China Normal University in Wuhan, China. He has published many books, including *Celebrity and Power* (Minnesota, 2014), *A Companion to Celebrity,* and *New Media Cultures,* along with the forthcoming *Contemporary Publics, Advertising, and Promotional Culture: Case Histories* and *Persona Studies.*